I CAN ONLY IMAGINE™

This journal is designed to take you on a journey through Jesus' encounters with broken people, found throughout the Gospels. Each day will include scripture, reflective questions, and prayer—all working together to reveal God's incredible heart for you.

Table of

Contents

INTRODUCTION

AND A VOICE FROM HEAVEN
SAID, "THIS IS MY SON,
WHOM I LOVE; WITH HIM I
AM WELL PLEASED."

— MATTHEW 3:17

How many of us long to hear those words—that we are deeply loved and fully accepted? We hope to hear these words from our friends, our siblings, and especially our fathers. But the need goes deeper. Whether we are aware of it or not, we all long to hear our heavenly Father saying, "You are my child; I love you, and I'm pleased with you!"

But how many of us feel and daily live with the sense of God's love and acceptance?

Jesus lived with this certainty: the love and acceptance of his eternal Father flooded his life, filled his conversations, and formed the basis for his teaching and ministry. Knowing you are loved by God changes everything!

We may not be like Jesus just yet, but all who believe in him are said to be "children of God" (1 John 3:1). As God's very own sons and daughters, we can be as certain as Christ of our Father's love and acceptance!

DISCOVERING THE FATHER'S LOVE

In the film, *I Can Only Imagine*, the life story of MercyMe lead singer Bart Millard is told for the first time. Bart grew up with an abusive father and a distant mother, and in early adulthood, came face to face with his own deep need for acceptance. His lack of love from his earthly father challenged his faith and hope in his heavenly Father.

But our God is in the business of re-demption—of working miracles. Bart's story mirrors so many of our own lives and gives fresh hope to those of us longing to hear the words, "With you, I am well pleased."

What does it look like to discover God's love and acceptance firsthand?

WALKING WITH JESUS THROUGH THE GOSPELS

In this study journal, we will take a four-week journey into the Father's heart. And the best way to discover God's heart is through the life and ministry of Jesus. Jesus' life demonstrates his eternal connection to the Father and best reveals the heart of God.

By walking with Jesus in the four Gospels—Matthew, Mark, Luke, and John—over 28 days, we will find the smiling face of God Almighty in the words and actions of his Son.

Imagine a loving Father. Imagine complete forgiveness. Imagine restoration to God and others. Imagine discovering your true home in the Lord.

God is love. Let's walk with Jesus through the Gospels to discover this life-changing reality.

HOW TO USE THIS JOURNAL

My hope and prayer for you is that this journal serves as a guide for your walk with Jesus into the Father's love.

Consider making this more than just another book, or another task to complete. Consider committing to a 28-day journey into the Father's heart!

This study journal has 28 days, including four days to catch up and review. That's four weeks saturated in the story of Jesus' life, a whole month of discovering God the Father in the face of God the Son.

Imagine what God might do in your heart and mind through this four-week journey with Christ!

Each day, you'll reflect on a portion of Scripture, stories, scenes from the 2018 film, *I Can Only Imagine*, and reflection questions to help you grow in your nearness to God.

If you're doing this journal with the *I Can Only Imagine* Series, watching each week's video BEFORE completing the Journal is recommended. For example, watch Episode 1, then complete Week 1 in the journal.

Watching the *I Can Only Imagine* movie is not necessary for completing this journal, but seeing Bart's story come to life in film will help you understand some of the illustrations given in this journal. We suggest watching the film before you start the journal if you choose to do so.

RECALL, REORIENT, REIMAGINE

Each week, we'll follow a pattern: Recall (days 1-2), Reorient (days 3-5), and Reimagine (days 6-7). This pattern can serve as an intentional guide to:

• **Recall** your own past through the stories of Bart Millard and of the Scriptures; by recalling the past with vulnerability, we can put the past "in its place"—neither dominating us nor unknown to us.

• **Reorient** to the present moment by finding our identity in Christ; by reorienting in the present with honesty, we can face our daily reality with faith, hope, and courage.

• **Reimagine** a better future; by reimagining a different future, we trust Christ to bring all things under his lordship and to guide us in each new season of life.

REFLECTION QUESTIONS

Each day, you'll read a short devotional based on Scripture and the themes of *I Can Only Imagine.*

Following the reading, you'll be asked to reflect on a series of questions. These questions are meant to cultivate a deeper understanding of the Scriptures' meaning and to help you experience God through prayerful reflection.

REMEMBER, WE READ AND REFLECT NOT MERELY TO LEARN. WE READ AND REFLECT TO EXPERIENCE.

The God of the universe—the Father of love and restoration—invites you to get to know him personally through his Word.

READING THE GOSPELS AS STORIES

Almost every devotional passage in this book is from one of the four Gospels—Matthew, Mark, Luke, or John. These passages give perspective on Jesus' life and meaning from other New Testament or Old Testament passages. As you read the passages from the Gospels, keep a few things in mind.

THE GOSPELS ARE STORIES.

The four firsthand accounts of Jesus' earthly life and ministry were written by his closest friends or most devoted followers. Each of the four books is primarily "narrative," the literary genre we know as stories full of meaning. Since many of these narratives span several verses and even chapters, in many cases, I will paraphrase sections of Scripture in my own language. My goal is to maintain a unified voice in retelling the stories in a fresh way, and I'll include as many Scripture references as possible.

THE GOSPELS ARE PERSONAL.

Jesus' ministry was often focused on one person at a time, and each of the four Gospels is intimately personal.

The stories invite us to imagine the scenes; the teaching may pierce our hearts, and the accounts of our Lord's death and resurrection may trigger strong emotions. In some cases, I may fill in the gaps with details to provide a personal reading. I won't make changes to Jesus' teachings, invent new characters, or make speculations beyond the biblical text. But to keep a unified voice and make your reading personal, I may fill in the gaps with reasonable reflections, and again, Scripture references will usually be included for your own reference and later study.

THE GOSPELS ARE POWERFUL.

These narratives from Jesus' life are not mere stories; they are passages from the divinely-inspired Word of God. I hope to preserve the power of God's Word throughout the study journal, supplementing the text only with reflections that honor the Scripture's integrity and magnify the most powerful moments in the narrative.

So, to summarize, in many cases I will take a particular verse and paraphrase it as a personal, powerful story that remains true to the biblical text, and I'll include the Scripture reference. For example:

THE ORIGINAL VERSE:

"When Jesus came down from the mountainside, large crowds followed him. A man with leprosy came and knelt before him and said, "Lord, if you are willing, make me clean." Jesus reached out his hand and touched the man. "I am willing," he said. "Be clean!"

- MATTHEW 8:1-3

MY PARAPHRASE:

When he had finished his teaching on the mountain, Jesus returned to the gritty realities of life in a broken world. Immediately, he was greeted by a sick man, a social outcast, who fell down at his feet. With nothing to lose and no fear of others' opinions of him, he wept before Jesus. "Lord, I believe you can heal me. Please, make me clean!" And so Jesus reached down, and to the crowd's dismay, touched the man—he hadn't felt the warmth of human touch in years. Smiling, Jesus said softly, "You are healed."

- MATTHEW 8:1-3 PARAPHRASE

I hope this form of biblical storytelling enhances your reading and gives you a greater love for Scripture. Some great examples of this form of narrative paraphrasing can be found in Sally Lloyd-Jones's *The Jesus Storybook Bible*, Eugene Peterson's *The Message Bible*, and Russ Ramsey's *Behold the King of Glory and Behold the Lamb of God*.

Questions for Reflection

Before starting Day One, complete these short Reflection Questions.

WHAT'S THE FIRST THING THAT COMES INTO YOUR MIND WHEN YOU THINK ABOUT GOD?

HOW WOULD YOU DESCRIBE GOD TO SOMEONE WHO DIDN'T KNOW ANYTHING ABOUT CHRISTIANITY?

REFLECT ON YOUR RELATIONSHIP WITH YOUR OWN FATHER. WHAT POSITIVE MEMORIES COME TO MIND? HOW HAVE YOU SEEN YOURSELF LONG FOR A PERFECT, HEAVENLY FATHER?

Call To Action

At the end of each week, you'll receive a Call to Action. This section moves beyond mere reflection and into immediate application. Some aspects will include reflection, but this section is action-oriented. You may find yourself journaling, writing a letter you never send, imagining a conversation, and other activities.

Before starting Day One, complete this short Call to Action.

IN THE SPACE PROVIDED, MAKE A LIST OF THREE THINGS YOU WANT TO GET OUT OF THIS STUDY.

PICK A PERSON WHO CAN PRAY FOR AND ENCOURAGE YOU WHILE YOU DO THIS STUDY. TAKE A MOMENT NOW TO CALL OR TEXT THEM, ASKING FOR THEIR PRAYER AND SUPPORT WHILE YOU COMPLETE THE FOUR-WEEK JOURNAL—OR EVEN ASKING THEM TO PARTICIPATE WITH YOU!

IMAGINE

a loving father

Day 1

FINDING GOD IN THE SCRIPTURES

I n *I Can Only Imagine*, Bart Millard's past became a defining and controlling factor in his life. In order to become spiritually healthy, he had to recall the past: his mother's absence, his father's abuse, and his own leaving. On some level, we can all resonate with Bart's past.

RECALLING THE PAST

Maybe your mother never left you; maybe your father never abused you verbally or physically; maybe you didn't run from home at first chance. But Bart's past is our past, because we all come from broken homes, live in a broken world, and bear the wounds of our own mistakes and the wrongs committed against us by others.

By recalling the past with vulnerability, we can put the past "in its place"; we can be neither dominated by the past nor unaware of its influence on us.

Why can't we just forget about the past and move forward?

God has hard-wired us as a remembering people. In fact, a memory of the past is central to biblical faith—the Scriptures are full of commandments to remember all that God has done for us. As people with full memories, we can't simply ignore or reject or forget the past; it's as if the past is woven into our bodies like our own DNA. To deny our own past is to put a lid on what God can do to bring about redemption and renewal in us. Spiritual growth requires a healthy recalling of our own past.

But there's another sense in which we must recall the past.

The biblical encouragements to "Remember" most often call us back, not to our own individual pasts, but to the past provision of God in history. Psalm 105 is a perfect example: The psalmist calls us to remember God's promises to Abraham, His saving work in the Passover and exodus, and in leading His people through the wilderness. Remembering these things, according to Psalm 105's conclusion, enables us to live rightly before God and others.

LOOK TO THE LORD AND HIS STRENGTH;
   SEEK HIS FACE ALWAYS.

Remember

THE WONDERS HE HAS DONE,
   HIS MIRACLES, AND THE JUDGMENTS HE
PRONOUNCED...

- PSALM 105:4-5

FINDING GOD IN THE SCRIPTURES

Each day in this study, we'll strive to find God in the Scriptures as a way of recalling our spiritual heritage. One of the best ways to discover God is to look to the earthly life and work of his own Son, Jesus Christ.

Use your imagination to recall the past:

What would it have been like to walk with Jesus in the first century—to work with him in Nazareth, to follow him along the dirt roads of Galilee, to sit across the table from him at a dinner in Jerusalem?

We can get some idea of what it would be like to be physically with Jesus by reading the stories of the Gospels, which were written by some of his closest friends and most loyal followers.

And as we put ourselves within the narratives of the gospels, we find Jesus inviting us into the heart of God.

THE SON REVEALS THE FATHER

JOHN 1 SAYS, "NO ONE HAS EVER SEEN GOD, BUT THE ONE AND ONLY SON, WHO IS HIMSELF GOD AND IS IN CLOSEST RELATIONSHIP WITH THE FATHER, HAS MADE HIM KNOWN."

- JOHN 1:18

Jesus, the Son of God, best reveals God, his eternal Father. As you prepare to study the life and ministry of Jesus, do you believe that God will reveal himself to you?

JESUS TOLD HIS DISCIPLES, THE FATHER HIMSELF LOVES YOU
BECAUSE YOU HAVE LOVED ME AND HAVE BELIEVED THAT I
CAME FROM GOD.

- JOHN 16:27

As you prepare to step into this four-week journey in the Gospels, do you believe that God himself loves you because you have believed in his Son?

In the words of Jesus' beloved disciple, "And so we know and rely on the love God has for us. God is love" (1 John 4:16). As you start this study journal, would you say that you know and rely on the love God has for you? Have you experienced this reality: God is love?

Perhaps you have never experienced love and acceptance from your father or mother. Perhaps you wonder if there's anyone who loves you unconditionally and accepts you just as you are. Perhaps this is God's invitation to you to discover, through the life of Jesus in the Gospels, just how deeply the Father loves you. ■

Questions for Reflection

READ JOHN 1:18 AGAIN. WHAT DOES IT MEAN THAT JESUS IS GOD AND IN RELATIONSHIP WITH THE FATHER? HOW IS JESUS UNIQUELY POSITIONED TO REVEAL THE FATHER TO US?

READ JOHN 16:27 AGAIN AS WELL. HOW IS GOD ABLE TO REVEAL HIS LOVE TO US? WHY IS IT NECESSARY THAT WE BELIEVE IN JESUS BEFORE WE CAN HAVE AN EXPERIENCE WITH GOD?

WHY IS IT NOTEWORTHY THAT THE SCRIPTURES COME TO US PRIMARILY IN STORY FORM—NOT JUST LAW AND TEACHING? WHAT DO YOU THINK GOD—AS THE ULTIMATE AUTHOR OF THE BIBLE—IS TELLING US BY HIS USE OF STORY?

HOW FAMILIAR ARE YOU WITH THE FOUR GOSPELS? WHEN WAS THE LAST TIME YOU READ ONE COVER TO COVER? WHICH OF THE FOUR BOOKS RESONATE WITH YOU MOST DEEPLY?

AS YOU START THIS STUDY JOURNAL, HOW WOULD YOU DESCRIBE YOUR RELATIONSHIP WITH GOD? HOW WOULD YOU DESCRIBE YOUR RELATIONSHIP TO HIS WORD, THE BIBLE?

THE APOSTLE JOHN SAYS, SIMPLY, "GOD IS LOVE" (1 JOHN 4:16). WHY IS THIS SO SIGNIFICANT? EVEN IF YOU'VE HEARD THIS PHRASE MANY TIMES IN YOUR LIFE, TAKE A MOMENT TO REFLECT ON IT DEEPLY. WHAT DOES IT MEAN TO YOU TODAY?

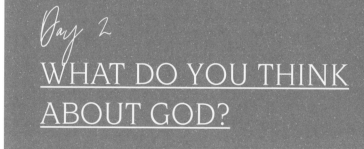

Day 2

WHAT DO YOU THINK ABOUT GOD?

For many of us, our view of God is based largely on our life experiences—particularly with our own fathers and mothers. By recalling truths about God and by recalling our own life experiences, we can become aware of who God is, how he has moved in our lives, and how his promises for future hope can be trusted.

The film *I Can Only Imagine* follows MercyMe lead singer Bart Millard's life story. Bart's mother left home while he was still a child. He was raised in a broken home by his angry and abusive father. It was a childhood of pain, abandonment, disillusionment, and brokenness.

WHAT DO YOU THINK ABOUT GOD?

A twentieth century pastor and author named A.W. Tozer once wrote,

"WHAT COMES INTO OUR MINDS WHEN WE THINK ABOUT GOD IS THE MOST IMPORTANT THING ABOUT US."

A.W. TOZER

Think about it: What comes into your mind when you think about God? What words, thoughts, phrases, images, promises, or experiences come to mind?

Next, consider: Why is your original thought about God so important? Why does what you think about God define you so deeply?

Our thoughts about God determine much more than how we view him—they reveal and determine how we will approach all of life. When Jesus walked this earth, he demonstrated an eternal connection to the Father and revealed the heart of God. By looking to Jesus—in his actions, in his teachings, and in how his closest friends characterized him—we find the most accurate picture of God.

WHAT IS GOD LIKE?

One of Jesus' closest friends and followers, the disciple John, would go on to write the Gospel of John, Revelation, and the three letters we know as 1, 2, and 3 John. These five books are excellent places to discover not just the life and teaching of Jesus, but how Jesus thought about his Father. Summarizing God's true character and ways, John wrote this:

DEAR FRIENDS, LET US LOVE ONE ANOTHER, FOR LOVE COMES FROM GOD. EVERYONE WHO LOVES HAS BEEN BORN OF GOD AND KNOWS GOD. WHOEVER DOES NOT LOVE DOES NOT KNOW GOD, BECAUSE GOD IS LOVE. THIS IS HOW GOD SHOWED HIS LOVE AMONG US: HE SENT HIS ONE AND ONLY SON INTO THE WORLD THAT WE MIGHT LIVE THROUGH HIM. THIS IS LOVE: NOT THAT WE LOVED GOD, BUT THAT HE LOVED US AND SENT HIS SON AS AN ATONING SACRIFICE FOR OUR SINS.

– 1 JOHN 4:7-10

So, what is God like?

FIRST, JOHN SAYS THAT GOD IS A FATHER.

By sending "his one and only Son," God demonstrates that fatherhood is central to his identity and being. He has eternally existed as a Father, and the Son, Jesus Christ, has eternally enjoyed the fellowship of a good and perfect Father.

SECOND, JOHN TWICE WRITES THE FAMOUS WORDS: GOD IS LOVE.

God is not simply loving or full of love; he is love. In other words, love is not the primary thing and God secondary; "love comes from God," meaning love can only be understood as an offspring of God's nature.

THIRD, JOHN TELLS US THAT GOD IS FOR US.

The Father did not wait for us to find our way to him; we could never make it on our own, not given our sin against him. God demonstrates his love for us—you and me and the whole world—by sending his only Son, so "that we might live through him." God is not against us. Quite the opposite: God is self-giving (he sacrificially gives what we need) and life-giving (we enter a new life by being "born of God").

What is God like? He is a Father; he is love; and he is for us.

IMAGINE A LOVING FATHER

Think back to Bart Millard's story. Even in a broken home, Bart was not beyond God's sight. Even his father, Arthur, the drunk and abusive older man, was not beyond God's grace. Although Bart didn't feel Arthur's acceptance and affection throughout his life, God would still reveal himself as the good and perfect Father to Bart—and to Arthur.

There are no prodigal sons too far from home. There are no fathers too poor to be changed by God.

Imagine a good, ever-present Father.
Imagine the God who is love.

Imagine: God is for you.

How could you not be transformed, encouraged, and strengthened by such a great God?

To help you better understand your view of God, go through the exercise on the next page. Remember, no one has a perfect image of God. We all hold false images of him, doubt his love for us at times, and question his ability to fully provide for us. But he nonetheless invites us to bring those false images, doubts, and fears to him. He already knows what's in our hearts and minds; bring these things before his throne of mercy and find healing in the love and power of his presence. ■

Exercise

Put a check mark next to the word, phrase, or image that you associate with God. Be as honest as possible.

☐ LOVE	☐ INDIFFERENT
☐ FATHER	☐ DEITY / RELIGION
☐ SAFE	☐ HARSH
☐ CLOSE	☐ DISTANT
☐ HAPPY	☐ ANGRY
☐ INVITING	☐ DEMANDING
☐ FULL OF GRACE	☐ HARD TO PLEASE
☐ FULL OF TRUTH	☐ DETACHED FROM REALITY
☐ FORGIVING	☐ UNFORGIVING
☐ REDEEMING	☐ NO SECOND CHANCES
☐ PROMISE KEEPING	☐ UNABLE TO PROVIDE
☐ PATIENT	☐ IMPATIENT

IN THE LEFT COLUMN, WHICH TRUTHS ABOUT GOD SEEM MOST NEAR TO YOU? HOW DID YOU COME TO TRUST GOD FOR THESE ATTRIBUTES OR CHARACTERISTICS?

IN THE RIGHT COLUMN, WHAT NEGATIVE IMAGES OF GOD HAVE YOU ADOPTED? HOW DID YOU DEVELOP THIS THOUGHT?

Questions for Reflection

IN 1 JOHN, THE APOSTLE SAYS, "GOD IS LOVE." WHY DO YOU THINK HE PUTS IT THIS WAY—NOT "GOD IS FULL OF LOVE" OR "GOD IS LOVING"?

HOW CAN IT BE THAT "WHOEVER DOES NOT LOVE DOES NOT KNOW GOD, BECAUSE GOD IS LOVE"? WHY IS IT IMPOSSIBLE TO LOVE FULLY APART FROM FIRST RECEIVING LOVE FROM GOD?

WHY DOES WHAT YOU THINK ABOUT GOD DEFINE YOU SO DEEPLY?

WHAT PEOPLE HAVE MOST INFLUENCED YOUR THOUGHTS ABOUT GOD?

THINK OF YOUR OWN EARTHLY FATHER: HOW DID HE RESEMBLE THE GOOD AND LOVING HEAVENLY FATHER—OR HOW DID HE FALL SHORT? HOW DOES YOUR RELATIONSHIP TO YOUR DAD AFFECT THE WAY YOU THINK ABOUT GOD THE FATHER?

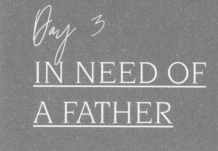

Day 3

IN NEED OF A FATHER

E ach week, we're following a pattern: recall, reorient, and reimagine. To reorient to the present moment means receiving and living, not in our past, but in our identity in Christ. By reorienting in the present with honesty, we can face our daily realities with faith, hope, and courage.

One of the primary spiritual "reorientations" that must take place involves seeking God as a good and loving Father. But we can't assume that finding God as Father is a naturally life-giving thought.

In America, millions of people grow up every year without knowing their father, with an absent father, or in a conflicted relationship with their father. David Blankenhorn has written:

> **"The United States is becoming an increasingly fatherless society. A generation ago, an American child could reasonably expect to grow up with his or her father. Today, an American child can reasonably expect not to. Fatherlessness is now approaching a rough parity with fatherhood as a defining feature of American childhood."**
>
> DAVID BLANKENHORN

IN NEED OF A GOOD AND LOVING FATHER

As a pastor for the last seven years, I have talked with countless men and women who were raised without a father. Although most still mature into fully-functional adults and contribute to society alongside everyone else, they often carry a deep "father hunger." In regular relationships and at work, they find themselves striving for others' approval, fearful of being abandoned, and doubtful that their own families will remain intact.

But fatherlessness is not limited to the literal absence of a father. Many grow up and live as adults with fathers who are neglectful or detached. There is a father, but he isn't present. When he is present, he doesn't make his presence felt. When his presence is felt, it's not full of affirmation and affection.

Similarly, others grow up with a father who was physically present but emotionally damaging. Perhaps you can vividly remember your father scolding you, punishing you cruelly for childish activity, embarrassing you in front of your peers, questioning your life plans, or expressing disappointment with you. Perhaps it's even a current reality, not a distant memory. Indeed, father wounds run just as deep as father hunger.

Fatherlessness is one of the great epidemics of our time.

We were all created to be cared for and provided for by a good father. In the Bible, fathers are called to be providers, care-givers, instructors, and models of holiness. But many people never experienced the affection, protection, and provision of a biblical father.

Mike Wilkerson, a counselor, has written:

> **"Tragically, for many of us the father-child relationship is fraught with fear, shame, dread, disappointment, or absence. For some of us… the word father has been darkened by the worst evils. Can you ever hope to know God as your Father if your view of father is so broken?"**

MIKE WILKERSON

What does it look like for those with a broken image of father to discover the true and better Father?

THE FATHER ATTENDS THE SON'S BAPTISM

As a father myself, I make it a point to attend my sons' important moments. Whether it's a baseball game, a school awards ceremony, or a show at the end of art camp, I want to be there whenever possible. My own dad was almost always present for my big days—first days of school, basketball games, my wedding, after the births of our children. Those are distinct memories for me.

In the same way, God the Father occasionally revealed himself to Jesus during his earthly ministry. In a much greater way than a dad's trip to the school gym, God shows up to his only Son's baptism, a defining moment that formally launches his earthly ministry of teaching and healing.

> Then Jesus came from Galilee to the Jordan to be baptized by John. But John tried to deter him, saying, "I need to be baptized by you, and do you come to me?" Jesus replied, "Let it be so now; it is proper for us to do this to fulfill all righteousness." Then John consented.

> As soon as Jesus was baptized, he went up out of the water. At that moment heaven was opened, and he saw the Spirit of God descending like a dove and alighting on him. And a voice from heaven said, "This is my Son, whom I love; with him I am well pleased."

– MATTHEW 3:13-17

How did God reveal himself as a good and loving Father at Jesus' baptism?

When Jesus was baptized, his Father was present. God was not absent from his eternal Son's baptism and he is not absent from your own life either.

The Father sent his Spirit to make his presence felt. God was not only present, he made sure his Son felt his presence; in the same way, God wants you to know and feel that he is always with you.

The Father spoke words of affirmation—"This is my Son... with him I am well pleased." God did not remain silent, but voiced his thundering affirmation of his Son: "I am pleased with you!" In the same way, we who are sons and daughters of God, take confidence that he is pleased with us too—not because we're perfect, but because we are one with Christ, and his perfect life covers our imperfect lives.

The Father expressed his love and affection—"This my Son, whom I love." God is not only affirming, he is affectionate. He loves his Son. Perhaps you remember many times your earthly dad said, "I'm proud of you." But how many times did you hear, "I love you"?

As he spoke over Christ, so our heavenly Father now speaks over all of his children, "You are my beloved!" ■

Questions for Reflection

WHY DID JESUS SAY HE NEEDED TO BE BAPTIZED BY JOHN? WHY DO YOU THINK IT'S SIGNIFICANT THAT JESUS WANTED TO BE BAPTIZED BEFORE THE START OF HIS TEACHING AND HEALING MINISTRIES?

HOW DOES MATTHEW 3:13-17 REFLECT THE TRUTH WE READ YESTERDAY, THAT "GOD IS LOVE" (1 JOHN 4:7-10)?

GOD RARELY SPEAKS IN AN AUDIBLE VOICE IN HUMAN HISTORY. WHY DO YOU THINK HE MADE AN EXCEPTION AND SPOKE LOUDLY OVER HIS SON IN THIS MOMENT? WHAT DOES THIS SAY ABOUT GOD AS A FATHER?

IF YOU THINK ABOUT GOD SIMPLY FROM THIS PASSAGE ALONE, WHAT ARE THE FIRST WORDS, THOUGHTS, PHRASES, OR IMAGES THAT COME TO MIND?

WHICH OF THESE REALITIES DO YOU FIND HARD TO BELIEVE? WHY DO YOU THINK THAT IS?

GOD IS PRESENT AND MAKES HIS PRESENCE FELT.

GOD AFFIRMS, ACCEPTS, AND LOVES YOU.

LASTLY, WRITE OUT THE END OF MATTHEW 3:13-17 IN YOUR OWN WORDS, WITH YOUR OWN NAME IN THE TEXT. FOR EXAMPLE, "THIS IS JEREMY, MY VERY OWN SON. I AM PROUD OF HIM. IN FACT, I LOVE HIM!"

Day 4
RETURNING HOME TO THE FATHER

Perhaps it is a struggle for you to think of God as a good and loving Father.

In *I Can Only Imagine*, Bart wanted nothing to do with his dad and left home as soon as he could. Even after years away, he couldn't imagine returning home to his father. Years later, Bart hit rock bottom and finally did arrive back home. When he did, he certainly didn't expect a transformed, loving dad. But God is full of surprises.

In one of his most famous stories, Jesus tells a parable—a fictional tale meant to convey a simple truth in a personal, powerful way—about a son who ran away from home. Perhaps you have read it many times. But consider the story again, in a paraphrased form.

THE RETURN OF THE PRODIGAL

Jesus once told this story to a crowd who struggled to see God as Father. "There was once a father who had two sons (Luke 15:11). The younger son wanted nothing to do with his dad, asked for his inheritance early—effectively wishing his father dead and breaking away from the family. Amazingly, the Father consented, sold off much of his assets, and let his son run away with his hard-earned life savings (v. 12).

So the younger son set off for the big city, spending

money like it would never run out. But it soon did. In fact, the economy bottomed out and he found himself broke and unemployed. The only job he could get was as a laborer on a farm—a worse position than those serving in his family's own house. But still his pride remained, and he was so desperate for food, he even tried the pig slop (v. 13-16).

Finally, he hit rock bottom. He couldn't do it anymore. His hard heart melted, and he knew his only way to stay alive—to truly live—was to go back home. As he walked the long road back, he rehearsed his apology speech over and over aloud. He knew he'd have to explain himself; he'd have to get his story just right (v. 17-20).

That's when he saw something totally unexpected: His father, dressed up in his work clothes, running toward him and waving his arms frantically. Before the son could get out a word of apology, his father tackled him, hugging him and sobbing uncontrollably (v. 20).

"Dad, I'm sorry..." the son began. But the father only shouted back to the family, "My son is home! My son is alive and he's home! Stop everything. Let's celebrate!" (v. 21-24).

THE FATHER'S LOVE

For many years, I thought this was a parable about the prodigal son—and it's about him to a degree. But it's really a story about the father. Think about it: Jesus wasn't telling his followers that they needed to turn from their lives of sin. If the son had been accepted back as a servant, a common laborer, as the son had hoped (v. 19), that would have made sense as a story about the son's change of heart. But the parable is not about getting it right and pulling it together. It's not about finding the right words to use or the right attitude to have.

THE PARABLE IS ABOUT THE LOVE OF THE FATHER.

"You're not my servant... You are my son!" the father responds (v. 24). Why would Jesus tell this story? What does he want his followers to think about God?

Jesus wants his followers—even you and me—to approach him just as we are, without getting our stories straight and cleaning the pig slop off our faces. He wants us to come home and receive his love. He's not looking for servants; he owns the cattle on a thousand hills (Psalm 50:10).

No, he's looking for his beloved children to come home. ■

"THE SON SAID TO HIM, 'FATHER, I HAVE SINNED AGAINST HEAVEN AND AGAINST YOU. I AM NO LONGER WORTHY TO BE CALLED YOUR SON.'

"BUT THE FATHER SAID TO HIS SERVANTS, 'QUICK! BRING THE BEST ROBE AND PUT IT ON HIM. PUT A RING ON HIS FINGER AND SANDALS ON HIS FEET. BRING THE FATTENED CALF AND KILL IT. LET'S HAVE A FEAST AND CELEBRATE.

FOR THIS SON OF MINE WAS DEAD AND IS ALIVE AGAIN; HE WAS LOST AND IS FOUND.'"

- LUKE 15:21-24

Questions for Reflection

WHAT IS THE MAIN MEANING OF THE PARABLE OF THE PRODIGAL SON? WHY DO YOU THINK JESUS TOLD THIS PARABLE?

HOW DO YOU SEE JESUS DEMONSTRATE GOD AS THE ULTIMATE FATHER IN THIS PARABLE IN THE FOLLOWING WAYS:

GOD IS PRESENT, AND MAKES HIS PRESENCE FELT.

GOD AFFIRMS, ACCEPTS, AND LOVES YOU.

IF YOU THINK ABOUT GOD SIMPLY FROM THIS PASSAGE ALONE, WHAT ARE THE FIRST WORDS, THOUGHTS, PHRASES, OR IMAGES THAT COME TO MIND?

IN WHAT WAYS DO YOU IDENTIFY WITH THE PRODIGAL SON? EVEN IF YOU HAVEN'T LIVED AN EXTRAVAGANT, OUTWARDLY BROKEN LIFE, HOW HAVE YOU RECOGNIZED THE FATHER'S ACCEPTANCE OF AND AFFECTION FOR YOU, DESPITE YOUR SIN?

If you find it hard to identify with the prodigal son, read the rest of the story—Luke 15:25-31.

WHAT IS DIFFERENT ABOUT THE OLDER BROTHER? HAVE YOU EVER FOUND IT HARD TO FORGIVE SOMEONE WHO HAS SQUANDERED SO MUCH OF THEIR LIFE? HOW DOES THE FATHER IN THE PARABLE DEMONSTRATE LOVE AND PATIENCE TO HIM AS WELL?

Day 5

OUR FATHER IN HEAVEN

ow do we reorient our lives around our heavenly Father? One way we refocus ourselves on the true God is by discovering how Jesus presents him to us through his teaching.

One day, Jesus and his disciples were being followed by a large crowd, so they went up on a mountainside (Matthew 5:1-2).

Just as Moses had ascended a mountain to receive God's Word—the Ten Commandments (Exodus 20)—so a new and better prophet was on the mountainside, giving a new and deeper Law.

"You have heard it said..." Jesus would often begin, but then—capturing the attention of his Jewish hearers—he would surprise them. "But I say to you..." he would continue (for example, Matthew 5:21).

Jesus wasn't giving a new Law, but he was personalizing it (Matthew 5:17-21). He was saying, in effect, "You thought you were good enough to keep this law... But your hearts aren't in the right place."

Throughout his teaching, Jesus was turning the world upside down: "Blessed are the poor in spirit... those who mourn... the meek... who hunger and thirst for righteousness..." (Matthew 5:2-6). The world values strength and independence; Jesus values weakness and dependence. The world values ambition and achievement; Jesus values the pursuit of humility and goodness.

But when he began to teach on prayer, he didn't flip us upside down. No, he taught us to, through prayer, turn our hearts right-side up.

APPROACHING THE FATHER

When you pray, Jesus told them, don't pray to impress others (Matthew 6:5-8). Instead, pray simply:

OUR FATHER IN HEAVEN...

Did you catch that? Jesus gives us permission to approach God directly—and as our Father! Having God as our Father means that we as his children, get regular, uninhibited access to him.

I remember seeing a picture of President Obama with his daughters when they were still young girls. They knew he had just become President, but to them, he was still just Dad. As his children, they had total access to him.

Imagine if you or I tried to get immediate access to the President. Unless you are a high-ranking government official, you most likely couldn't get an appointment. And if you didn't have an appointment, the Secret Service would certainly stop you if you got too close on your own. But the President's children don't need an official position in the Cabinet; they don't need an appointment; they don't even need a good reason to see him. They can simply walk right up to him, jump on his lap, distract him from his work, and enjoy his company. They are his children! Children have regular, complete, uninhibited access to their father.

How great it is to be a child of the Most High God! How wonderful to have regular, complete, uninhibited access to the most powerful, most patient, most loving Being in the cosmos. Simply put, we can approach him wherever we are, no matter what we've done, with no hint of fear. He is our Father.

When we realize who God is and how much he loves us, our whole lives can be reordered around his life-giving presence.

Remember the disciple John, one of Jesus' closest friends? This is how he puts it:

SEE WHAT GREAT LOVE THE FATHER HAS LAVISHED ON US, THAT WE SHOULD BE CALLED CHILDREN OF GOD. AND THAT IS WHAT WE ARE!

- 1 JOHN 3:1

HOW DEEP THE FATHER'S LOVE FOR US

God has lavished his love on us by calling us his own sons and daughters. But John also tells us that God's love is most fully visible not in receiving us, but in how much he had to give to receive us back. Since every one of us has broken God's law and broken our relationship with God, the Father had to make a way for us to be restored—he had to give his own beloved Son up to death. John writes:

THIS IS HOW WE KNOW WHAT LOVE IS: JESUS CHRIST LAID DOWN HIS LIFE FOR US.

- 1 JOHN 3:16

Take a moment now to read and reflect on the lyrics from the hymn "How Deep the Father's Love for Us." ∎

How Deep The Father's Love for Us

Words and Music by
Stuart Townend

♩ = 54

G   **Am** **G/B** **C**   **G/B**   **G/D** **D**

1 How   deep   the   Fa - ther's   love   for us,   how   vast   be - yond   all   meas - ure   That
2 Be - hold   the   Man   up - on   a   cross,   my   sin   up - on   His   shoul - ders.   A -
3 I   will   not   boast   in   an - y - thing: no   gifts,   no   pow'r,   no   wis - dom.   But

3   **G**   **Am** **G/B** **C**   **G/B**   **D**   **G**

He   should   give   His   on - ly   Son   to   make   a   wretch   His   treas - ure.   How
shamed,   I   hear   my   mock - ing   voice   call   out   a - mong   the   scof - fers.   It
I   will   boast   in   Je - sus   Christ: His   death   and   res - ur - rec - tion.   Why

5   **Am** **G/B**   **C**   **G/B**   **Em**   **D**

great   the   pain   of   sear - ing   loss.   The   Fa - ther   turns   His   face   a - way   As
was   my   sin   that   held__   Him   there   un - til   it   was   ac - com - plished;   His
should   I   gain   from   His__   re - ward?   I   can - not   give   an   an - swer.   But

7   **G**   **Am** **G/B** **C**   **G/B**   **D**

wounds   which   mar   the   Cho - sen   One   bring   man - y   sons   to   glo -
dy - ing   breath   has   brought   me   life.   I   know   that   it   is   fin -
this   I   know   with   all   my   heart: His   wounds   have   paid   my   ran -

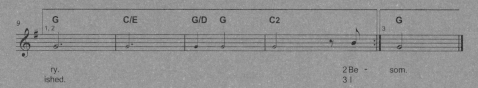

9   1, 2   **G**   **C/E**   **G/D** **G**   **C2**   3   **G**

ry.
ished.   2 Be -   som.
        3 I

CCLI Song #1558110

Questions for Reflection

WHY DO YOU THINK JOHN EMPHASIZED
BECOMING CHILDREN OF GOD AN ASPECT
OF OUR SALVATION?

HOW DOES JESUS STARTING THE FAMOUS
LORD'S PRAYER WITH "OUR FATHER"
CHANGE THE WAY YOU THINK ABOUT IT?

HOW DOES THE DEATH AND
RESURRECTION OF JESUS DEMONSTRATE
THE LOVE OF GOD?

REFLECT ON THE LYRICS OF THE HYMN ON P.45. HOW DOES LOOKING TO THE CROSS—JESUS' CRUCIFIXION, BURIAL, AND RESURRECTION—GIVE YOU INCREASED LOVE FOR GOD? HOW DOES JESUS' SACRIFICE FACTOR INTO YOUR DAILY LIFE?

WHAT DOES IT LOOK LIKE FOR YOU TO EMBRACE GOD AS A GOOD, PRESENT, LOVING FATHER TODAY?

Day 6

ADOPTED BY GOD

This week, we've been learning a new pattern of spiritual renewal: recall, reorient, and reimagine. Once we have recalled our past, and after reorienting ourselves to the truths about God in Scripture, we can reimagine a better future with God.

By reimagining a different future, we trust Christ to bring all things under his lordship and to guide us in each new season of life.

For instance, we have already looked at the remarkable reality that we are sons and daughters of God through faith in Jesus (1 John 3:1). But how are we made children of God? Through adoption! By reimagining our own adoption, we discover much about who God is—and who we are as well.

For [God] chose us in [Christ] before the creation of the world to be holy and blameless in his sight. In love, he predestined us for adoption to sonship through Jesus Christ, in accordance with his pleasure and will—to the praise of his glorious grace, which he has freely given us in the One he loves. (Ephesians 1:4-6)

WHAT DOES IT MEAN TO BE ADOPTED?

Some close friends of mine are in the process of adopting a child. Their desire is to become parents through adoption, to offer a home and a family to a child that has neither. One day soon, they will have a child—most likely, a young boy or girl from a broken home within their state—offered to them for adoption. They will be able to choose to adopt this child, and at that point, the boy or girl would legally become their own son or daughter.

Think about the spiritual analogies.

IN ADOPTION, AN ORPHAN IS GIVEN A FAMILY AND A HOME.

As we saw yesterday, Jesus invites us to approach God as Father—with regular, uninhibited access. But our adoption also gives us a family and a home. The Church becomes our brothers and sisters in Christ. Imagine being adopted in to a large family: Children all from different backgrounds, different languages, different worldviews, all of a sudden thrust into one house together.

That's the church. No wonder it's both amazing and wonderful, and exceedingly difficult. There will always be challenges of living in a family of different backgrounds, but we can all recognize that none of us were anything when God chose us, so we can relate to one another with humility and love.

IN ADOPTION, OUR STATUS AS SONS AND DAUGHTERS IS PERMANENT.

As a dad myself, there are times when my young children disobey my directions, talk back to me in anger, or—in the recent case of my three-year old—throw Legos at me. I don't like their behavior, but I don't stop loving them. They're being children, and this disobedience is an unfortunate stage of their development. I certainly don't stop being their dad.

In the passage above, Paul writes, "In love, he predestined us to sonship" (Eph. 1:5). Think about how marvelous this is! (Set aside any disagreements over predestination.) God chose us to

49

be his sons and daughters before we were born—knowing full well how much we would sin, how often we would rebel, and how much patience we would require. And he adopted us anyway. This is God's way of saying: "I gave everything to get you: It took years of effort and a huge cost for us to get you. There's no way we're turning back now!"

IN ADOPTION, THERE IS A HIGH COST TO THE PARENTS AND NO COST TO THE CHILD.

We are heirs of Christ's Kingdom. In adoption, we become legal, official sons and daughters of God. It's a permanent decision. Imagine being adopted into a very wealthy family: As a full member of the family, you receive a share from your parents' riches, and you have those riches permanently. You didn't earn them, you didn't work for them; but they do legally belong to you through union. In the same way, everything that belongs to Christ now legally and permanently gets credited to your account.

Adoption comes at an enormous cost to the parents. What does this adoption cost the child? Nothing —"in accordance with the grace freely given us in the One he loves... in accordance with the riches of God's grace lavished on us" (Ephesians 1:6-8).

THE AVERAGE ADOPTION IN THE U.S. IS ABOUT $40,000.

It required the sacrifice of Jesus on the Cross. Adoption came at a grace cost to the Father.

In adoption, a parent chooses to welcome the child into their family not because of anything the child has done or proven, but simply out of love.

We were adopted by God for the same reason that any parent adopts—out of sheer love. We are adopted "in love" and "to the praise of his grace" (Ephesians 1:4-6). God is not just full of love; God is love. Love is just an expression of God being God.

In his great love, he plans adoption, pays the cost, becomes our Father, unites us to a whole family of brothers and sisters, offers us his immeasurable wealth, and gives us the assurance that nothing can separate us from him. ■

Once adopted, you belong to the Father forever.

Questions for Reflection

WHICH ASPECT OF ADOPTION SEEMS MOST SIGNIFICANT TO YOU? WHICH SPIRITUAL PARALLEL SEEMS MOST POWERFUL?

HOW DOES ADOPTION CHANGE THE WAY YOU THINK ABOUT GOD AS YOUR FATHER?

IF YOU THINK ABOUT GOD SIMPLY BASED ON HIS ADOPTION OF YOU, WHAT ARE THE FIRST WORDS, THOUGHTS, PHRASES, OR IMAGES THAT COME TO MIND?

READ AND REFLECT ON EPHESIANS 1:4-6 AGAIN. WHAT IS THE SIGNIFICANCE OF THE PHRASE "IN LOVE…"? DO YOU HESITATE TO BELIEVE THAT GOD LOVES YOU?

IS THERE ANYONE IN YOUR LIFE WHO WOULD BE BLESSED AND ENCOURAGED TO KNOW THAT GOD IS THEIR FATHER, THAT THEY HAVE A NEW SPIRITUAL FAMILY, AND THAT THEY ARE DEEPLY LOVED IN CHRIST? REACH OUT TO THEM TODAY!

Day 7

CALL TO ACTION

O n the seventh day of each week, we're going to pause to review and reflect on the past week, and then we'll move forward with a Call to Action (see Introduction).

If you are behind a day or two, use this day to catch up. If you are caught up, use this day to review the previous six days' notes—especially all the Scripture references and stories.

Based on your week's reading and reflection, answer the following questions..

Recall

WHAT WAS THE MOST SIGNIFICANT THING YOU LEARNED ABOUT GOD THIS WEEK?

WHAT HAVE YOU LEARNED ABOUT YOURSELF THIS WEEK?

Reorient

WHAT WAS THE MOST SIGNIFICANT THING YOU LEARNED ABOUT THE CHRISTIAN LIFE THIS WEEK?

WHAT DOES IT LOOK LIKE TO REORIENT YOUR LIFE AROUND THE REALITY OF GOD AND HIS LOVE FOR YOU?

Reimagine

WHAT WOULD YOUR LIFE LOOK LIKE IF YOU FULLY BELIEVED EVERYTHING YOU READ ABOUT GOD'S FATHERLY LOVE FOR YOU THIS?

HOW MIGHT YOUR LIFE BE DIFFERENT AFTER A TRANSFORMATIVE EXPERIENCE WITH GOD? IF YOU HAVEN'T HAD A TRANSFORMATIVE EXPERIENCE, DESCRIBE WHAT MIGHT BE HOLDING YOU BACK.

Call To Action

In the space provided or in your own notebook, write a letter to your father. You don't necessarily need to send the letter, so be as honest as possible.

HOW ARE YOU THANKFUL FOR HIM? WHERE DID HE FAIL YOU OR HURT YOU? WHAT DOES IT LOOK LIKE TO FORGIVE HIM?

I Can Only Imagine

Verse 1

I CAN ONLY IMAGINE
WHAT IT WILL BE LIKE
WHEN I WALK,
BY YOUR SIDE
I CAN ONLY IMAGINE
WHAT MY EYES WILL SEE
WHEN YOUR FACE
IS BEFORE ME
I CAN ONLY IMAGINE
I CAN ONLY IMAGINE

Verse 2

I CAN ONLY IMAGINE
WHEN THAT DAY COMES
WHEN I FIND MYSELF
STANDING IN THE SON
I CAN ONLY IMAGINE
WHEN ALL I WILL DO IS FOREVER
FOREVER WORSHIP YOU
I CAN ONLY IMAGINE
I CAN ONLY IMAGINE

Chorus

SURROUNDED BY YOUR GLORY,
WHAT WILL MY HEART FEEL?
WILL I DANCE FOR YOU JESUS
OR IN AWE OF YOU BE STILL?
WILL I STAND IN YOUR PRESENCE
OR TO MY KNEES WILL I FALL?
WILL I SING HALLELUJAH,
WILL I BE ABLE TO SPEAK AT ALL?
I CAN ONLY IMAGINE
I CAN ONLY IMAGINE

IMAGINE

forgiveness

Day 8

THE LORD OF FORGIVENESS

L ast week, we discovered a helpful pattern: We can *Recall* our past (days 1-3), *Reorient* to the present (days 4-5), and *Reimagine* a better future (days 6-7).

IMAGINE FORGIVENESS

This entire week, we'll look at the theme of forgiveness in the life and ministry of Jesus.

Today, we will recall how Jesus forgave people and taught his followers to forgive. At the same time, we'll recall ways in which we have each been forgiven. We'll discuss our role in forgiveness later in the week, but until we recall how much we've been forgiven of, we won't be able to reorient around fully forgiving others through Christ.

APPROACHING CHRIST

Consider an amazing example of forgiveness from Mark 2.

A FEW DAYS LATER, WHEN JESUS AGAIN ENTERED CAPERNAUM, THE PEOPLE HEARD THAT HE HAD COME HOME. THEY GATHERED IN SUCH LARGE NUMBERS THAT THERE WAS NO ROOM LEFT, NOT EVEN OUTSIDE THE DOOR, AND HE PREACHED THE WORD TO THEM.

SOME MEN CAME, BRINGING TO HIM A PARALYZED MAN, CARRIED BY FOUR OF THEM. SINCE THEY COULD NOT GET HIM TO

JESUS BECAUSE OF THE CROWD, THEY MADE AN OPENING IN THE ROOF ABOVE JESUS BY DIGGING THROUGH IT AND THEN LOWERED THE MAT THE MAN WAS LYING ON.

- MARK 2:1-4

Use your imagination to recall this story with fresh eyes and ears. At this point in Jesus' earthly ministry, he has become so popular that people would travel long distances to see him, hear him teach, and make their own decision about him. Here, Jesus is teaching in a large house, and some loyal friends bring their paralyzed friend to the event.

The four friends are here to help their long-suffering brother. The paralyzed man himself may not have expected much from Jesus, but the friends were unfazed by the crowds and the full house. They were not going home! So they climbed on the roof, carrying their friend up on a mat. After cutting a hole through the roof, they tied the man to his mat and slowly lowered him down.

Can you imagine this? What would you do if you were in church or at a public lecture, and someone opened the roof and lowered down a paralyzed person? Would you think the men behind this mischief were crazy?

These four men had incredible faith: This was no ordinary religious service or lecture. This was Jesus!

He was their one hope for healing.

JESUS FORGIVES AND HEALS

WHEN JESUS SAW THEIR FAITH, HE SAID
TO THE PARALYZED MAN,

"SON, YOUR SINS ARE FORGIVEN."

NOW SOME TEACHERS OF THE LAW
WERE SITTING THERE, THINKING TO
THEMSELVES, "WHY DOES THIS FELLOW
TALK LIKE THAT? HE'S BLASPHEMING!
WHO CAN FORGIVE SINS BUT GOD
ALONE?"

IMMEDIATELY JESUS KNEW IN HIS SPIRIT
THAT THIS WAS WHAT THEY WERE
THINKING IN THEIR HEARTS, AND HE
SAID TO THEM, "WHY ARE YOU THINKING
THESE THINGS? WHICH IS EASIER: TO
SAY TO THIS PARALYZED MAN, 'YOUR
SINS ARE FORGIVEN,' OR TO SAY, 'GET
UP, TAKE YOUR MAT AND WALK'?

- MARK 2:5-9

Did you notice that there was no mention of forgiveness till this point? What a strange response by our Savior! The paralyzed man came for healing, but Jesus looked directly into his heart and saw his true need. The man's greatest problem was not the brokenness of his body, but the brokenness of his heart. He didn't just need physical healing; he needed spiritual healing.

Perceiving the religious leaders' disgust, Jesus poses a question. While the audience is trying to figure out how to respond—and what to make of this unusual event and Jesus' perplexing response—Jesus speaks again.

HEALING FORGIVENESS

"But I want you to know that the Son of Man has authority on earth to forgive sins." So he said to the man, "I tell you, get up, take your mat and go home." He got up, took his mat and walked out in full view of them all. This amazed everyone and they praised God, saying, "We have never seen anything like this!" (vv. 10-12)

To prove the inner transformation that has just taken place in the paralyzed man, Jesus offers physical transformation: "Get up and go home!" So the man left after, not one, but two miracles. His body was healed and his sins were forgiven.

He had truly been given a second chance at life! Imagine the crowd's cheering! Imagine the healed man's joy! Imagine the story he could now tell the rest of his life. "Jesus healed me— inside and out!" ■

Questions for Reflection

WHAT PART OF THIS STORY SURPRISED YOU MOST? WHAT DOES THIS PASSAGE TELL YOU ABOUT GOD'S DESIRE FOR FORGIVENESS?

HOW WOULD YOU DESCRIBE THE PARALLELS BETWEEN HEALING AND FORGIVENESS? WHY DO YOU THINK JESUS ADDRESSED BOTH NEEDS—AND IN THE ORDER THAT HE DID?

Think of a time in life when you desperately needed to be forgiven. Maybe you spoke out in anger against your coworker, spouse, or child. Perhaps you made decisions at work or with your finances that were improper. Maybe it's your life before Christ, living completely apart from God's law.

WHAT DID IT FEEL LIKE TO NEED FORGIVENESS?

IN WHAT WAYS DID YOUR OTHER NEEDS (PHYSICAL, ETC.) THREATEN TO TAKE THE FOCUS OFF YOUR MOST SIGNIFICANT DEBT (THE SPIRITUAL)?

DO YOU OFTEN THINK BACK ON THE FORGIVENESS YOU'VE RECEIVED FROM CHRIST OR ANOTHER PERSON? WHY OR WHY NOT?

WHY DO YOU THINK WE OFTEN HAVE SUCH A HARD TIME ADMITTING OUR NEED OF FORGIVENESS?

Day 9

FACING FORGIVENESS

I n *I Can Only Imagine*, Bart Millard's past was a defining and controlling factor in his life. His mother had left when he was a young boy. His father, Arthur, had neglected Bart, abused him verbally and physically, and doubted his ability to make a living as a musician.

Bart left home thinking his father would never change. In fact, Arthur himself didn't think he could change. But God would prove both of them wrong!

RECALLING THE PAST

Bart tried living his life without reflecting on his past. He tried to move on, to form a new life, to escape his past. But he eventually had to face his past—just as we all must do.

When traveling with his band, Bart finally came to his end. Frustrated with poor reviews from record executives, he lashed out in a rage that resembled his own father's anger. Bart's band was terrified.

In a quiet moment, Bart faced his own past. His manager's question rung in his mind:

"WHAT ARE YOU RUNNING FROM?"

The manager knew what Bart was just realizing: You can't run from the past unaffected. It was time to go home.

But could Bart forgive his father?

LEARNING FORGIVENESS

Jesus led his disciples to a green hillside and sat down (Matthew 5:1-2). Surrounded by his own disciples and an exterior crowd of onlookers, he began to teach. Jesus was not concerned with external appearances of religious obedience; he was after his followers' internal transformation. While teaching his disciples to pray, he came to the exceedingly difficult topic of forgiveness:

> OUR FATHER IN HEAVEN,
> HALLOWED BE YOUR NAME...
> FORGIVE US OUR DEBTS,
> AS WE ALSO HAVE FORGIVEN OUR DEBTORS.
>
> — MATTHEW 6:9,12

Why does forgiveness play such a central role in the famous Lord's Prayer? Jesus knew his followers would be tempted to embrace a "spiritual" life without facing the messy realities of life in a broken world. True spirituality, Jesus seems to be teaching, has forgiveness at its core. Moments later, Jesus added:

> FOR IF YOU FORGIVE OTHER PEOPLE WHEN
> THEY SIN AGAINST YOU, YOUR HEAVENLY
> FATHER WILL ALSO FORGIVE YOU. BUT IF YOU
> DO NOT FORGIVE OTHERS THEIR SINS, YOUR
> FATHER WILL NOT FORGIVE YOUR SINS.
>
> — MATTHEW 6:14-15

Now this is a provocative statement: God will only forgive those who forgive others! Could it be true? Considering these words come directly from Christ—and they are also echoed in Mark 11:25 and John 20:23—we must believe these words and obey.

It wouldn't be a stretch to say that this is one of the most demanding of all Jesus' teachings.

Exercise

Think of someone who has hurt you, neglected you, or sinned against you in some way. Although it may be painful, recall how this person or event wounded you.

First, go to the Father in prayer. Ask the Father to give you a soft, forgiving heart. You may write out your own prayer or use the one on the next page:

RECALL

FATHER GOD,

I believe you have forgiven me from so much sin. I have sinned against you and against others. Yet you don't hold that sin against me, but forgive me and call me 'righteous' in Christ. Thank you for such mercy! Now, will you give me the grace to forgive _____ as I have been forgiven? You know how much I have been hurt by _____ But their sin against me is not so great as my sin against you. So Father, I forgive _____ Give me wisdom to express my forgiveness.

Now, it may be wise to write a note or make a phone call to express this forgiveness or seek healing in the relationship. ▪

Questions for Reflection

WHAT IS YOUR INITIAL GUT RESPONSE TO JESUS' TEACHING ABOUT FORGIVENESS? WHY DO YOU THINK IT'S OFTEN SO DIFFICULT TO FORGIVE OTHERS?

HOW DOES BART'S ANGER TOWARD HIS DAD RESONATE WITH YOU? OR HOW HAVE YOU SENSED YOUR OWN ANGER WITH THE PAST DEBILITATING OR LIMITING YOU IN THE PRESENT?

HOW MIGHT YOU ANSWER THE QUESTION, "WHAT ARE YOU RUNNING FROM?"

Consider Titus 3:3-6 below.

HOW DOES THE GOOD NEWS OF OUR SALVATION MOVE YOU TO PRAISE AND GRATITUDE?

WHEN THE KINDNESS AND LOVE OF GOD OUR SAVIOR

APPEARED, HE SAVED US, NOT BECAUSE OF RIGHTEOUS

THINGS WE HAD DONE, BUT BECAUSE OF HIS MERCY.

HE SAVED US THROUGH THE WASHING OF REBIRTH AND

RENEWAL BY THE HOLY SPIRIT, WHOM HE POURED OUT ON US

GENEROUSLY THROUGH JESUS CHRIST OUR SAVIOR.

- TITUS 3:3-6

Day 10

THE FORGIVENESS PRINCIPLE

I n *I Can Only Imagine*, Bart Millard's past became a defining and controlling factor in his life. In order to become spiritually healthy, he had to recall his mother's absence, his father's abuse, and his own leaving. On some level, we can all relate with Bart's past.

RECALLING THE PAST

Maybe your mother never left you; perhaps you were never abused or neglected as a child. Praise God!

But we have all been hurt in the past. We have all felt neglected, underappreciated, and lonely. We have all failed to respond perfectly to these pains. What does it look like to recall the past and find healing?

Forgiveness enables us to find restoration from our own sins and from the sins of others committed against us.

We must receive God's forgiveness.

We must forgive those who have hurt us.

We must become "ambassadors of forgiveness" in a world of grudges and resentment.

FORGIVEN TO LOVE

In Luke 7, Jesus is eating dinner with Pharisees and other religious leaders when a highly-questionable woman walks in. The

Scriptures describe her as "a woman who had lived a sinful life" (v. 37), meaning her very identity is tied to her sin against God and others. Yet she approaches Jesus.

Her actions are shocking: She kneels before Jesus. She begins to cry. Weeping openly, she uses her tears to cover the feet of Jesus.

Then she does the most shocking thing of all: She breaks open her jar of perfume—likely her most valuable possession—and begins to clean the feet of the Lord. Kissing Jesus' feet, the unnamed woman wipes his feet clean with her own hair—completing a sort of anointing ritual for the Son of God (v. 38).

Jesus doesn't reject her, doesn't embarrass her, doesn't ask her to come back later. He simply receives her affection as true worship. In fact, in a room full of good, religious people, she is the only one acting appropriately in his presence.

THE FORGIVENESS PRINCIPLE

Sensing the religious leaders' dismay, Jesus tells a parable. A wealthy man had loaned money to two of his friends. Put in contemporary terms, one friend owed him $50,000, and the other owed $5,000. But neither friend could pay back the loan, so the wealthy man forgave both debts.

Jesus, turning to his good friend Simon Peter, asks, "Which friend will love him more?" Peter answers the way we all would: "Probably the one who had the bigger debt forgiven" (v. 43).

Jesus turns the room's attention to the woman who had lived a sinful life. Jesus points out that this woman has shown him hospitality; this woman has served his needs; this woman has shown him affection (v. 44-46). "Her many sins have been forgiven—as great as her love has shown" Jesus says. Turning up the pressure, he states the powerful moral to his parable, a sort of forgiveness principle. "Whoever has been forgiven little loves little" (v. 47).

THE FORGIVENESS PRINCIPLE:

Whoever has been forgiven little loves little.
Whoever has been forgiven much loves much.

SO WHO ARE YOU?

The forgiveness principle begs the question: Who are you? Have you been forgiven little? Or, before a holy God, have you been forgiven much?

In *I Can Only Imagine,* Bart struggles to forgive his father. Having returned home to a transformed person, Bart says, "God can forgive you. I can't."

If you are not sure if you have much to be forgiven for, consider the decades of your thoughts, motives, and actions. If that's not enough, consider what you may have failed to do for others that you should have or could have done.

THE REALITY IS THAT WE HAVE ALL BEEN FORGIVEN FROM A MOUNTAIN OF SIN.

Instead of what's fair, we have received generosity. We have received lavish grace. And to the extent that we understand what we've been forgiven from, we will return love to God. If we think we could have saved ourselves, we won't deeply love God. If we think others have been forgiven of much more than us, we will fail to love correctly.

But if we see ourselves as that sinful woman, if we believe we are ones "who have lived a sinful life," then what great love will arise within us!

It was only when Bart began to realize how much he had been forgiven that he was able to forgive and truly love his own father.

Recalling the forgiveness of God enables us to reorient around his grace and reimagine a life of love.

WHOEVER HAS BEEN FORGIVEN MUCH LOVES MUCH. ■

Questions for Reflection

HOW DOES JESUS' PARABLE—AND THE FORGIVENESS PRINCIPLE—ENCOURAGE OR CHALLENGE YOU? WITH WHOM DO YOU MOST IDENTIFY WITH IN THE STORY (PETER, THE PHARISEES, THE WOMAN)?

HOW MIGHT YOU INCREASE YOUR UNDERSTANDING OF THE FORGIVENESS YOU HAVE RECEIVED FROM GOD AND OTHERS? HOW DO YOU THINK THIS GREATER AWARENESS WOULD CHANGE YOU?

IN WHAT SITUATIONS OR RELATIONSHIPS
DO YOU IDENTIFY WITH BART'S
STATEMENT: "GOD CAN FORGIVE YOU; I
CAN'T"?

HOW IS JESUS INVITING YOU TO RECEIVE
HIS FORGIVENESS AND APPROACH HIM
LIKE THE SINFUL WOMAN?

Day 11

AMBASSADORS OF FORGIVENESS

You may remember the tragedy. On June 17, 2015, Emanuel African Methodist Episcopal Church gathered for their regular evening prayer service in Charleston, South Carolina. But a young man, with stated racist motivations, entered the church and opened fire, killing nine individuals and injuring three others.

In the days following the mass shooting and the gunman's arrest, I remember feeling a number of emotions, including anger and grief. I imagined what it would be like to lose a family member, friend, or pastor in that moment. I thought of all the ways this young man should be punished for his sinful crime. Of all these thoughts and emotions, there was only one response I didn't consider—

Immediate & total forgiveness.

RADICAL FORGIVENESS

In a news conference held at the killer's trial, the members of Emanuel AME Church came forward to offer forgiveness.

Nadine Collier, who lost her mother, 70-year-old Ethel Lance, said, "I forgive you. You took something very precious from me. I will never talk to her again. I will never, ever hold her again. But I forgive you. And have mercy on your soul."

"I acknowledge that I am very angry," said Bethane Middleton-Brown, whose sister, DePayne

Middleton-Doctor, died in the shooting. "But one thing that DePayne always enjoined in our family... is she taught me that we are the family that love built. We have no room for hating, so we have to forgive. I pray God on your soul."

Even a year later, Nadine Collier remained forgiving—despite being told by many that her forgiveness was unnecessary and a sign of weakness. She wasn't forgiving the killer because she had to, but because she was compelled by her faith. "Forgiveness is power. It means you can fight everything and anything head on."

Similarly, Bethane repeated a year later: "God is taking me to a higher level. If the man who killed my sister was looking for hate, he came to the wrong place."

What gave the Emanuel members this kind of powerful ability to forgive? The members of Emanuel Church weren't overlooking sin; they understood that they were sinful themselves and saved by grace alone.

AMBASSADORS OF FORGIVENESS

In a world of grudges and resentment, the Emanuel members are great representations of forgiveness. The apostle Paul wrote that we are now agents of forgiveness.

> GOD... RECONCILED US TO HIMSELF THROUGH CHRIST AND GAVE US THE MINISTRY OF RECONCILIATION: THAT GOD WAS RECONCILING THE WORLD TO HIMSELF IN CHRIST, NOT COUNTING PEOPLE'S SINS AGAINST THEM. WE ARE CHRIST'S AMBASSADORS, AS THOUGH GOD WERE MAKING HIS APPEAL THROUGH US.
>
> —2 CORINTHIANS 5:19-20

Since God has forgiven us and restored us to himself through Christ, we now join him in his work of forgiveness and reconciliation. We are ambassadors of forgiveness.

Have you ever thought about what an ambassador does? The United States employs ambassadors to most other nations of the world. Nominated by the President and Senate, ambassadors of the U.S. represent the nation in a foreign land. They speak on behalf of the President, build local relationships, and make decisions based on the President's best interests in the local community.

SPEAK
ON BEHALF

As Christ's ambassadors, we exist to represent Jesus in all areas of life on earth. In a world in which we are foreigners and exiles (1 Peter 2:11), we speak and make decisions as local representatives of Christ.

And if we are ambassadors of Christ, what did he teach about forgiveness? Once, Peter asked Jesus, "How many times shall I forgive my brother or sister who sins against me? Up to seven times?"

Jesus answered, "I tell you, not seven times, but seventy-seven times" (Matthew 18:21-22).

As Jesus' agents in this world, we can offer total and immediate forgiveness to those who sin against us. In so doing, it is "as though God were making his appeal through us."

Christ employs us as his ambassadors of

forgiveness

to invite the world

to share in his grace! ■

Questions for Reflection

**HOW DOES THE EMANUEL MEMBERS'
FORGIVENESS ENCOURAGE OR
CHALLENGE YOU?** HOW DO YOU THINK
YOU WOULD RESPOND TO SUCH AN
ABSOLUTE TRAGEDY?

**ARE THERE CIRCUMSTANCES WHERE
YOU THINK TOTAL AND IMMEDIATE
FORGIVENESS IS WRONG OR UNJUST?**

WHAT DO YOU THINK HAPPENS TO US WHEN WE RESIST FORGIVING OTHERS? HOW DOES THIS AFFECT OUR RELATIONSHIP WITH GOD AND OTHERS?

WHAT DOES IT LOOK LIKE FOR YOU TO EMBRACE YOUR CALLING AS AN AMBASSADOR OF FORGIVENESS TO THE WORLD? WHAT PEOPLE, RELATIONSHIPS, OR SITUATIONS COME TO MIND?

Day 12

FORGIVENESS AT THE CROSS

How do we reorient our lives around forgiveness?

In *I Can Only Imagine,* Bart Millard struggled to forgive his father, and his hurt disabled him from becoming healthy and whole. He was right to feel hurt and anger toward his father, but he was unable to find joy and peace until he could truly forgive.

As we have already read, we can only forgive others deeply when we realize how much we have been forgiven. But how do we know that we have been completely forgiven?

FORGIVENESS FROM THE CROSS

When Jesus' ministry on earth was nearly complete, he prepared his disciples for his death and resurrection. Though they didn't fully understand it at the time, he was about to give his life for them in the ultimate act of love and forgiveness.

Luke 23 describes the scene of Jesus' trials before Herod and Pilate. Jesus was questioned (v. 3), blamed (v. 5), accused (v. 10), ridiculed and mocked (v. 11). Though no charge was found against him, he was given the death penalty (v. 22). He was physically abused (v. 26) and verbally harassed (v. 35-37).

How did Jesus respond to all of this?

He never gave in to their accusations. He never raised his voice or spoke out in anger. He never defended himself. He willingly went to the cross.

He was hung on a wooden cross between two common criminals. One criminal joined the crowds in insulting him, but the other had a different response. "We are punished justly," the dying criminal admitted, "for we are getting what our deeds deserve. But this man has done nothing wrong" (v. 40-41).

Then, turning to Jesus with his last breaths, the man said, "Jesus, remember me when you come into your glory" (v. 42). And Jesus responded with a word of forgiveness—and possibly with a smile. "Truly I tell you: Today you will be with me in paradise" (v. 43).

As he was being mocked and ridiculed by the crowds—in the midst of agonizing pain and piercing loneliness—Jesus spoke out over the crowd. "Father, forgive them, for they know not what they are doing" (v. 34).

Even from the Cross, our sinless Savior's final words were of forgiveness. Father, forgive them.

THE ULTIMATE ACT OF FORGIVENESS

The crucifixion of Jesus Christ is the defining act of forgiveness in the entirety of human history.

Here's what I mean: No other sin committed has been as great as mankind's rejection of Christ. No other punishment given has been as severe as crucifixion. And no other pain experienced has been as great as Jesus' temporary loss of fellowship with his Father (Mark 15:34). But even still, Jesus offered forgiveness to us.

If we have received forgiveness at the Cross, then, there is no forgiveness we can offer that is too great.

THE PARABLE OF THE UNFORGIVING SERVANT

In response to Peter's question of repeated forgiveness, Jesus told this story (Matthew 18:23-35). A king wanted to settle his accounts with many servants who owed him money. One man owed him "ten thousand talents" (v. 24). Do you know how much money ten thousand talents was? A talent was the equivalent of twenty years' wages—basically the amount that was typically earned during one's adult years. So, this servant was in debt to his king ten thousand talents, meaning he owed 200,000 years of work.

Jesus' point in this parable is that the servant owed an amount no one could ever pay.

But when the servant begged his king for mercy, the king "canceled the debt and let him go" (v. 27). Total and immediate forgiveness!

How did the servant receive this great news? Unfortunately, the servant was not transformed by the forgiveness he had received. He went out, found a fellow servant who owed him a relatively small amount, and demanded payment. When the man with the small debt begged for mercy, the servant—who had just been forgiven of ten thousand lifetimes of debt—threw him in prison.

As Jesus concludes the parable, he calls the unforgiving man a "wicked servant" (v. 32), and states that our heavenly Father will reject any of us who don't "forgive [our] brother or sister from the heart" (v. 35).

Like the first servant in the parable, we have been forgiven of ten thousand lifetimes of debt. How can we now not forgive those who have relatively insignificant debts against us?

If we have received forgiveness from the Cross—if Christ laid down his very life to free us from our lifetime of sins—how can we not forgive one another from the overflow of our hearts? ∎

REORIENT

IN THE SHADOW OF THE CROSS,

WE FIND THE POWER OF

TOTAL

AND COMPLETE

forgiveness.

Questions for Reflection

READ THROUGH THE ACCOUNT OF JESUS' TRIALS, CRUCIFIXION, AND DEATH IN LUKE 23. WHAT STANDS OUT TO YOU FROM THE CROWD'S TREATMENT OF CHRIST? WHAT IS MOST IMPACTFUL FROM JESUS' RESPONSES?

HOW WOULD YOU DESCRIBE FORGIVENESS IN LIGHT OF JESUS' SACRIFICE?

**WHAT DO YOU THINK OF THE PARABLE
OF THE UNFORGIVING SERVANT?** HOW
DO YOU RESPOND TO JESUS' CLOSING
STATEMENT THAT ANY WHO FAIL TO
FORGIVE OTHERS WILL RECEIVE THE SAME
TREATMENT FROM GOD?

Day 13

TOO FAR FROM GOD?

This week, we have recalled the importance of forgiveness from Scripture and personal experience, and we have reoriented around the forgiveness we have received from God through Jesus and our call to be ambassadors of forgiveness.

Today and tomorrow, we will reimagine the power of a life of forgiveness and grace. How might we envision and enact the way of radical forgiveness?

TOO FAR FROM GOD?

We often think some people are too far from God.

In *I Can Only Imagine*, Bart Millard left home thinking he would never see his father again. He thought Arthur was hopeless, lost, unable to change.

When Bart Millard finally returned home years later, he couldn't believe Arthur's transformation was legitimate. And he struggled to forgive the man who had caused him such pain. But through their time together—over breakfast, working on their old truck, and listening to music—they began to build a new relationship. It turned out Arthur was not beyond God's saving power, and even Bart would discover a powerful picture of the Lord's relentless pursuit of us.

Consider another story Jesus told (Luke 15:1-7; Matthew 18:12-14).

A good shepherd counts the sheep in his flock and notices one of the lambs is missing. Ninety-nine are there, but the shepherd is concerned for the one.

So he leaves the ninety-nine on the hills and goes searching for that lost one. When he finds it, he rejoices and throws an extravagant party with his friends.

What's the message of this parable? Jesus concludes: "In the same way, your Father in heaven is not willing that any one of these little ones should perish" (Matthew 18:14). And at the recovery of a single lost child, all of heaven rejoices (Luke 15:7).

In other words, no one is too far from God. No one can run so far, rebel so greatly, or resist so strongly that God cannot save them. If the Lord has his eyes set on his child, he will not sleep till his missing child is home, safe and sound.

The reality of God's saving power also means that none of our friends or family members are too far from God either. We shouldn't ever give up on someone simply because they seem distant from or rebellious toward God. He works miracles, and we can persist in loving others in the same way that God does.

As Jesus himself said, "the Son of Man came to seek and to save the lost" (Luke 19:10).

REIMAGINE LIFE WITH GOD

How does this enable us to reimagine life with God? Ours is not a God who is quick to anger or slow to forgive. We don't have to run from him, we don't have to hide our sin, and we don't have to fear his judgment. For all who believe in Christ: We are his children, and he will stop at nothing to see us restored to him.

Do you live like this?

How might your life look different if you knew you had nothing to hide, no one to impress, and nothing to prove? If you knew you were forgiven and covered by the righteousness of Christ, how would daily life be different?

Imagine a good and loving father. Imagine total and immediate forgiveness. Imagine redemption—not just the removal of sin but a completely new life. Imagine going home. ∎

Exercise

Take a few minutes to finish the following statements and reflect on how God is inviting you to deeper intimacy with him.

IF I TRULY BELIEVED I HAVE BEEN FORGIVEN FROM ALL OF MY SIN...

IF I TRULY BELIEVED I AM A BELOVED CHILD OF GOD...

IF I TRULY BELIEVED NO ONE IS TOO FAR FROM GOD...

IF I TRULY BELIEVED I HAVE NOTHING TO HIDE OR PROVE...

IF I TRULY BELIEVED ALL HEAVEN REJOICES OVER ME...

Questions for Reflection

WHAT ABOUT THE THEME OF
FORGIVENESS MOST RESONATES WITH
YOU IN BART'S STORY, OR IN THE MOVIE
I CAN ONLY IMAGINE?

REMEMBER THE FORGIVENESS PRINCIPLE—
THAT THOSE WHO ARE FORGIVEN MUCH
WILL LOVE MUCH. BASED ON THE LOVE
YOU DEMONSTRATE TOWARD OTHERS,
HOW WOULD YOU RATE YOUR OWN
UNDERSTANDING OF YOUR FORGIVENESS?

**WHAT COMES INTO YOUR MIND WHEN YOU
HEAR THE PARABLE OF THE LOST SHEEP?**
DO YOU IDENTIFY MORE AS THE MISSING
SHEEP, THE ONES LEFT BEHIND, OR THE
SHEPHERD IN THE STORY? WHY SO?

Day 14
<u>CALL TO ACTION</u>

O n the seventh day of each week, we're going to pause to review and reflect on the past week, and then we'll move forward with a Call to Action (see Introduction).

If you are behind a day or two, use this day to catch up. If you are caught up, use this day to review the previous six days' notes—especially all the Scripture references and stories.

Based on your week's reading and reflection, answer the following questions.

Recall

WHAT WAS THE MOST SIGNIFICANT THING YOU LEARNED ABOUT GOD THIS WEEK?

WHAT HAVE YOU LEARNED ABOUT YOURSELF THIS WEEK?

Reorient

WHAT WAS THE MOST SIGNIFICANT THING YOU LEARNED ABOUT THE CHRISTIAN LIFE THIS WEEK?

WHAT DOES IT LOOK LIKE TO REORIENT YOUR LIFE AROUND THE REALITY OF GOD AND HIS LOVE FOR YOU?

Reimagine

WHAT WOULD YOUR LIFE LOOK LIKE IF YOU FULLY BELIEVED EVERYTHING YOU READ THIS WEEK?

HOW MIGHT YOUR LIFE BE TOTALLY DIFFERENT AFTER A TRANSFORMATIVE EXPERIENCE WITH GOD?

Call To Action

In the space provided or in your own notebook, write a letter to someone who has hurt you. Recall how they harmed, neglected, or mistreated you. Describe how that affected your heart. Now, write a few paragraphs offering forgiveness to them.

WHY DO YOU FORGIVE THEM? (WHAT ABOUT THE CROSS, OR THE LIFE OF JESUS, OR THE POWER OF FORGIVENESS ENABLES YOU TO FORGIVE NOW?)

I Can Only Imagine

CONSIDER READING OR SINGING ALONG TO THE LYRICS OF "I CAN ONLY IMAGINE" BY MERCYME.

Verse 1

I CAN ONLY IMAGINE
WHAT IT WILL BE LIKE
WHEN I WALK,
BY YOUR SIDE
I CAN ONLY IMAGINE
WHAT MY EYES WILL SEE
WHEN YOUR FACE
IS BEFORE ME
I CAN ONLY IMAGINE
I CAN ONLY IMAGINE

Verse 2

I CAN ONLY IMAGINE
WHEN THAT DAY COMES
WHEN I FIND MYSELF
STANDING IN THE SON
I CAN ONLY IMAGINE
WHEN ALL I WILL DO IS FOREVER
FOREVER WORSHIP YOU
I CAN ONLY IMAGINE
I CAN ONLY IMAGINE

Chorus

SURROUNDED BY YOUR GLORY,
WHAT WILL MY HEART FEEL?
WILL I DANCE FOR YOU JESUS
OR IN AWE OF YOU BE STILL?
WILL I STAND IN YOUR PRESENCE
OR TO MY KNEES WILL I FALL?
WILL I SING HALLELUJAH,
WILL I BE ABLE TO SPEAK AT ALL?
I CAN ONLY IMAGINE
I CAN ONLY IMAGINE

IMAGINE

redemption

Day 15
IMAGINE
REDEMPTION

n *I Can Only Imagine,* Bart and Arthur join together to fix their old truck. Arthur, in struggling health, notices an old trait in his son, and asks, "You like fixing what's been broken. What do you call that?"

Bart responds, "Redemption."

Initially, Bart could not believe the changes that were taking place in Arthur's life. But as he discovered that God was working a miracle in his father, Bart found a new depth to the meaning of redemption.

WE LONG FOR REDEMPTION

Redemption is the act of having freedom purchased or wholeness restored through a significant payment. Consider how we use the word in contemporary language:

We redeem a gift card—we receive the gift of someone else's payment.

A family experiences redemption when their goods are returned after a robbery.

A home mortgage fully paid off is considered redeemed.

An old piece of furniture fully restored has undergone redemption.

Redemption is a prominent theme in our own culture's stories and art. Novels, poems, and movies all contain the theme, often in their own title. Home restoration shows demonstrate physical redemption; dramas capture the power of redemptive relationships;

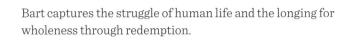

Bart captures the struggle of human life and the longing for wholeness through redemption.

We seem to naturally understand our own brokenness and so are attracted to the themes of redemption, reconciliation, restoration, and reclamation.

As human beings made in God's image and wrecked by our own sin and the brokenness of the world, we are hard-wired to long for redemption. As C. S. Lewis once wrote,

> **"If we find in ourselves a desire for which there is no worldly satisfaction, the most reasonable explanation is that we were made for another world."**

— C. S. LEWIS

REDEMPTION IN SCRIPTURE

Of course, redemption is first and foremost the work of God to restore his people to himself through the life, death, and resurrection of Jesus Christ.

Redemption occurred throughout the Old Testament, serving as foreshadowing for the coming of God's own Son.

God promises Moses and Israel freedom from Egypt, saying,

> "I WILL FREE YOU FROM BEING SLAVES TO THEM, AND I WILL REDEEM YOU WITH AN OUTSTRETCHED ARM AND WITH MIGHTY ACTS OF JUDGMENT"
>
> - EXODUS 6:6

When Boaz claimed Naomi out of destitution to become his wife, it was said,

> "PRAISE BE TO THE LORD, WHO HAS NOT LEFT YOU WITHOUT A REDEEMER!"
>
> - RUTH 4:14

Looking forward to the coming Messiah, the prophet Isaiah writes

> "BURST INTO SONGS OF JOY TOGETHER... THE LORD HAS REDEEMED JERUSALEM"
>
> - ISAIAH 52:9

THE LORD OF REDEMPTION

The redemption prophesied in the Old Testament came to fullness in the life and ministry of Jesus Christ.

When Jesus was born, the priest Zechariah said, "Praise be to the Lord, the God of Israel, because he has come to his people and redeemed them" (Luke 1:68).

The apostle Paul summarizes Jesus' ministry: "God sent his Son... to redeem those under the law, that we might receive adoption" (Galatians 4:4-5).

At the end of the age, Revelation described eternal worship where God's people "redeemed from the earth" (Revelation 14:3).

When God decided it was time to forgive his people's sins and draw them back to himself, he sent his one and only Son. Indeed, it was a redemption! At great cost to the Father and the Son (his own death!), our redemption was purchased and secured (Ephesians 1:14). In joy, this redemption is applied to us through the Holy Spirit as we believe in Christ (Ephesians 4:30). And once we are redeemed, we are adopted into a new eternal family (Galatians 4:5) and never go back into slavery (Hebrews 9:12).

As Paul summarizes in Titus 2:14:

> CHRIST "GAVE HIMSELF FOR US TO REDEEM US FROM ALL WICKEDNESS AND TO PURIFY FOR HIMSELF A PEOPLE THAT ARE HIS VERY OWN, EAGER TO DO WHAT IS GOOD." ■

Questions for Reflection

Take a moment now to pause and recall your own redemption—including forgiveness of sin, salvation, oneness with Christ, being filled with the Holy Spirit, and joined to the Church.

Answer the questions with deep reflection. Write a few sentences for each question:

BEFORE YOUR REDEMPTION, WHAT WERE YOU LIKE?

HOW WOULD YOU DESCRIBE YOUR PROCESS OF REDEMPTION?

WHAT WAS THE MOMENT YOU FELT REDEMPTION FULLY OCCURRED?

WHAT PEOPLE (FRIENDS, FAMILY) DID GOD
USE TO SECURE YOUR REDEMPTION?

HOW ARE YOU DIFFERENT NOW, HAVING
BEEN REDEEMED BY CHRIST?

Day 16

STORIES OF REDEMPTION

Yesterday, we recalled the meaning of redemption and saw how God has been working redemption for his people from the beginning to the end of human history. We discovered how redemption is fully accomplished in the life, death, and resurrection of Jesus: Through Christ, we are redeemed from our sins and fully restored to God.

Jesus is the Lord of redemption, and the four Gospels can be read as "stories of redemption." Throughout Matthew, Mark, Luke, and John, narratives abound on the theme of redemption.

For all of us who long for restoration and renewal, we find great joy and peace in walking with Jesus through the Gospels—his stories of redemption.

HE IS WILLING TO REDEEM

Matthew 8 tells the following story: When Jesus had finished teaching his famous Sermon on the Mount, large crowds followed him down. Surely he was exhausted from teaching, and surely not too much more should be asked of him. Right?

We often hesitate to come to Jesus when we are in need. We might think we are too broken; we may think Jesus isn't concerned with our small problems; we might not want to "bother" him with the messy parts of our lives. But he is willing to redeem.

A man with leprosy came and knelt before Jesus (v. 2). Lepers in Jesus' day througout Israel were considered unclean and had to keep a certain distance from others. If a leper touched you, you would become ceremonially unclean—meaning you had to be isolated for an amount of time and couldn't return to the temple for worship for even longer. You can imagine Jesus' disciples and the crowds disdained this man with leprosy for coming right up to Jesus.

Kneeling before Jesus, the man with leprosy begged, "Lord, if you are willing, you can make me clean." He was not afraid to approach Jesus. He knew others would be angry—perhaps even Jesus' own followers. It was a risk. But for this man, leprosy was a life sentence, and he had nothing to lose.

TOUCHED BY JESUS

When the leper asked Jesus for healing, he probably was hoping for a word of healing. Jesus often healed with just one word. And Jesus did speak: "I am willing. Be clean!" (v. 3).

But that was not what the sick man needed most. See, a man with leprosy in the first century, being totally isolated from society, would go years, even decades without human touch. They were often removed from their friends and family, and there was no compassionate medical care.

With a sick, leprous man kneeling before him, Jesus could have healed with just his words, but that's not what he did.

"Jesus reached out his hand and touched the man" (v. 3).

Imagine the man's surprise when Jesus took him by the hand, put his hand on his shoulder, touched his dry, white, sore-covered skin. Imagine the crowd's shock and concern: Jesus just touched a leper! Was Jesus now unclean? Did he not know the religious rules?

Or was Jesus high and above all religious rules? When Jesus touches the sick and lonely, he doesn't become unclean. The sick and lonely become clean and whole.

Immediately the man was cleansed of his leprosy. He had felt the compassionate, healing touch of Jesus. "Go and show yourself to the priest," Jesus told him, in keeping with tradition for restoration to community (v. 4).

REDEMPTION'S TOUCH

A man was sick. He was alone. He was unable to heal himself. It was an embarrassing condition; he had not felt loving, human touch in decades. He had one chance with Jesus, and he didn't waste it. In faith, he knelt before the Lord of redemption and asked for healing, for redemption.

Jesus doesn't just make us a little bit better. He doesn't improve our already-pretty-good health and spirituality. No, we were condemned, lonely, and unclean, and Jesus made us righteous, whole, and clean—able to stand before priests and kings without fear.

Jesus doesn't stand off at a distance from us, offering laws and principles and healing without touch. He could have healed without touching the leper, and he probably could have redeemed us without leaving his heavenly throne. He certainly could have saved us without being born in a dirty stable and growing up poor.

But that's not the Jesus of Scripture. Jesus Christ entered our dying, broken world. He walked on our grass and ate our food. Why? Because Jesus longs to become one with us.

At the heart of redemption, Jesus identifies with us—touches us in our moment of total uncleanness—and invites us into an encounter with him, to a real relationship with him. ■

Questions for Reflection

WHAT ABOUT THE THEME OF REDEMPTION MOST RESONATES WITH YOU IN BART'S STORY?

REMEMBER THE FORGIVENESS PRINCIPLE— THAT THOSE WHO ARE FORGIVEN MUCH WILL LOVE MUCH. HOW DOES THIS PRINCIPLE ENLARGE YOUR JOY IN REDEMPTION?

HOW DO YOU STRUGGLE TO IDENTIFY WITH THE CHARACTERS IN JESUS' LIFE—THE MAN WITH LEPROSY, THE RURAL POOR, HIS FRIENDS WHO LEFT HIM AT HIS MOMENT OF NEED? YET HOW ARE YOU ENCOURAGED THAT JESUS STILL IDENTIFIES WITH YOU?

HOW DO YOU SENSE JESUS INVITING YOU TO JOIN HIM IN HIS HEALING WORK OF REDEMPTION? WHO IN YOUR LIFE COULD USE A TOUCH OF REDEMPTION?

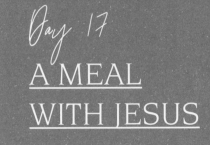

Day 17

A MEAL WITH JESUS

There's something powerful about connecting with someone over a meal.

When Bart returned home, he was startled awake by the smell of a warm breakfast. His father, Arthur, was not normally up before him—let alone cooking breakfast. Bart was even more surprised to find that his dad had learned to make a frittata and made two for breakfast. But then Bart's surprise nearly went through the roof as Arthur led them through an honest, simple prayer to bless the meal.

Meals are often a means of redemption. In a shared meal, two or more people take the time to slow down, prepare food together, and sit across and beside one another in fellowship. Eating together is an intentional breaking of barriers between people. Children build friendships through sitting together at lunch. Co-workers build relationships by going out for dinner after work. Government officials nego-tiate treaties over meals. In fact, our English word "companion" comes from two Latin words meaning "bread" and "together."

Meals can enact or embody the power of redemption and reconciliation between others.

Over the last two days, we recalled the meaning of redemption—how Jesus redeems us through the healing power of his personal touch. Today, we'll discover another "story of redemption" in our walk with Jesus through the Gospels.

EATING WITH JESUS

Jesus was often found eating with people.

Jesus' public ministry began with his miracle at Cana—turning barrels of water into wine at a wedding. He spent his time eating with "sinners and tax collectors," receiving gifts from marginalized women, encouraging widows, playing with children, and attending all major cultural events and parties.

Matthew writes, "The Son of Man came eating and drinking" (Matthew 11:19). Jesus seems to be eating throughout all four Gospel narratives. Consider examples from Luke alone:

JESUS...

eats with tax collectors and sinners at Levi's house (Luke 5).

is anointed at the home of a Pharisee during a meal (Luke 7).

feeds five thousand people (Luke 9).

eats in the home of Mary and Martha (Luke 10).

condemns the Pharisees and religious leaders over a meal (Luke 11).

urges people to invite the poor to their meals, not just their friends (Luke 14).

invites himself to dinner with Zaccheus (Luke 19).

gathers his disciples in the upper room for the Last Supper (Luke 22).

Jesus, risen from the grave, asks for a plate of fish (Luke 24).

One commentator notes, "Jesus is either going to a meal, at a meal, or coming from a meal." Another scholar jokes Jesus "eats his way through the Gospels."

DINNER WITH TAX COLLECTORS AND SINNERS

Mark 2 tells the story of an unforgettable meal with Jesus. Jesus had just called Levi, son of Alphaeus (who later was renamed Matthew), to be his disciple. After Jesus' invitation—"Follow me," he said (v. 14)—Levi invited Jesus over to his house.

Levi had been a tax collector, one of the most despised vocations in the Jewish world. Tax collectors were Hebrews employed by the Roman government, who heavily taxed Israel to keep them in submission to the Empire. To make matters worse, tax collectors were allowed to collect additional taxes to keep for themselves, so tax collectors were often crooked, negotiating higher taxes to make a profit themselves.

It's natural that when Levi became a follower of Jesus, he invited all of his friends—tax collectors and others considered serial sinners—to join him at his house for dinner.

Imagine the dinner crowd: Jesus, some of his closest followers, a rowdy crowd of outcasts and thieves, and the religious leaders watching from the outside (v. 15). The Pharisees seemed to gather a crowd of their own outside, pointing to Jesus' choice in companions and asking aloud, "Why does he eat with tax collectors and sinners?" (v. 16).

Jesus responded, "It is not the healthy who need a doctor, but the sick. I have not come to call the righteous, but sinners" (v. 17).

Why would Jesus eat with these outsiders? Jesus' meals are physical demonstrations of the salvation he offers to those who don't deserve it—to people like you and me.

JESUS INVITES US,

JUST AS WE ARE,

TO THE TABLE OF

redemption. ■

Questions for Reflection

IMAGINE SITTING DOWN FOR A MEAL WITH THE PERSON WHO HAS HURT YOU, DISAPPOINTED YOU, OR MISTREATED YOU MOST SEVERELY. HOW WOULD YOU ACT? WHAT WOULD BE GOING THROUGH YOUR MIND?

IMAGINE NOW WHAT IT WOULD BE LIKE TO SHARE A MEAL WITH JESUS. IMAGINE HIM SURROUNDED BY THREE GROUPS: YOUR OWN FRIENDS, SOME WILD TAX COLLECTORS AND SINNERS, AND RELIGIOUS LEADERS AND PHARISEES. HOW DO YOU THINK THAT MEAL WOULD PLAY OUT?

JESUS HAS INVITED YOU TO THE TABLE OF REDEMPTION. AS A DINNER GUEST, WHAT WOULD YOU WANT TO ASK HIM? WHAT DO YOU DESIRE IN YOUR RELATIONSHIP WITH HIM?

WHO HAS GOD PLACED IN YOUR LIFE THAT COULD BE INVITED TO A REDEMPTIVE MEAL AT YOUR OWN DINNER TABLE? WHO DO YOU KNOW THAT NEEDS TO HEAR THE MESSAGE OF GOD'S REDEMPTIVE PLAN?

Day 18
RESTING IN
REDEMPTION

This week, we have recalled the power of the redeeming touch of Christ. Now, we can reorient our hearts around the redemption we have received from God through Jesus and rest in his healing presence.

Too often, we don't take the time and energy to rest in what God has provided. Our world moves fast, and the culture tells us that resting is weakness or laziness. Similarly, we think we need to prove ourselves by our ability to perform well and are constantly comparing ourselves to one another.

But the Good News of redemption frees us from performance and comparison. Redemption says, "The pressure is off!" Redemption reorients us to rest in who God has made us to be in Christ.

GREATER THAN THE SABBATH

Consider another story of redemption in our walk with Jesus through the Gospels. In Matthew 12, Jesus was traveling by foot with his disciples on the Sabbath. Remember, God's fourth commandment prohibited his people from working on the Sabbath, but didn't give a specific set of instructions about what constituted work. Instead, the law was meant to be a blessing to us, that we might learn to trust God and not ourselves (Exodus 20:8-11).

But in Jesus' time, the Pharisees and other religious leaders had imposed additional laws around the fourth commandment. *(The Talmud, a book longer than the Old Testament, expounded on Hebrew law, creating additional laws for the people to live by.)* Within these extra laws, cooking, sewing, writing, carrying an object from one place to another, planting seeds, and picking grain were all included on the restricted list. Even putting out a fire was prohibited on the Sabbath.

Now, back to our story: Jesus and his disciples walked through a grain field on the Sabbath, and they picked a few heads of wheat and ate them. Not surprisingly, the Pharisees nearby called them out, commanding them not to pick grain on the Sabbath.

Jesus' response is powerful. He said, "Something greater than the temple is here... [and] the Son of Man is Lord of the Sabbath" (v. 6-8). Two of the religious leaders' most beloved institutions—the temple and the Sabbath—were not created to oppress God's people but to liberate us. In fact, all of God's laws exist for our good (Psalm 119:39).

So these religious places and activities—consider even praying, resisting temptation, and gathering with your church—are gifts from Jesus for our good. He is greater than the temple and Lord of our laws.

His redemption enables us to put religion in its place, and most importantly, to reorient our lives around the rest that he provides.

WE DON'T HAVE TO WORK ALL SEVEN DAYS
BECAUSE WE ARE NOT SOVEREIGN OVER
THE WORLD—

HE IS.

WE DON'T HAVE TO GET THE LAW
PERFECTLY RIGHT—

HE ALREADY HAS.

WE DON'T HAVE TO TRY TIRELESSLY
TO PLEASE HIM—

WE CAN REST IN HIM.

HEALING AND REST

As the story continues, Jesus and the disciples enter a synagogue for Sabbath worship, and the Pharisees remain close at hand—like police officers ready to hand out tickets to an unruly mob. At the synagogue, a man with a crippled hand approaches Jesus. Trying to condemn Jesus, the Pharisees ask him if it is lawful to heal on the Sabbath (v. 10). Of course, their man-made laws prohibited it. So Jesus does what he often did to turn the tables on religious people: He tells a story!

> "IF ANY OF YOU HAS A SHEEP AND IT FALLS INTO A PIT ON THE SABBATH, WILL YOU NOT TAKE HOLD OF IT AND LIFT IT OUT? HOW MUCH MORE VALUABLE IS A PERSON THAN A SHEEP! THEREFORE IT IS LAWFUL TO DO GOOD ON THE SABBATH."
>
> - MATTHEW 12:11-12

Jesus catches them in their foolishness. The Talmud had restricted medical care, but there was no specific provision against miraculous healing. So Jesus invited the man to stretch out his hand, and immediately it was completely restored—"as sound as the other" (v. 13).

REDEEMED: SET FREE!

Jesus' redemption does not come with the introduction of another law or demand. His teaching is light and his way is accessible (Matthew 11:28-30). His redemption isn't slavery to another way; it's true freedom, complete liberation. This story is not simply about the Sabbath—or even healing. It is another reminder that *our redemption is complete.* As Jesus announced:

"THE SPIRIT OF THE LORD... HAS SENT ME TO PROCLAIM FREEDOM FOR THE PRISONERS AND RECOVERY OF SIGHT TO THE BLIND, TO SET THE OPPRESSED FREE, TO PROCLAIM THE YEAR OF THE LORD'S FAVOR."

- LUKE 4:18-19

In *I Can Only Imagine,* Bart received a gift of freedom: His father provided for him financially to let him focus on his dream. The payments would allow Bart to write "I Can Only Imagine." In a similar way, we have received riches from our heavenly Father, and with that freedom, we can fully be ourselves.

This is redemption: Christ has come to set "the burdened and battered free" (Luke 4:18, The Message).

When Jesus sets us free, we are free indeed! Perhaps for you—even now—this is the moment of the Lord's favor. ■

OUR *redemption* IS COMPLETE

Questions for Reflection

WHEN YOU THINK ABOUT REST—OR
PERHAPS TAKING A DAY OFF EACH WEEK—
WHAT COMES INTO YOUR MIND?

WHY DO YOU THINK JESUS WAS SO
WELCOMING AND PATIENT WITH THE POOR,
THE SICK, AND OTHER OUTSIDERS, YET SO
DIRECT AND DEMANDING TOWARD THE
RELIGIOUS LEADERS?

IF YOU FULLY AND COMPLETELY EMBRACED YOUR REDEMPTION, HOW DO YOU THINK YOU MIGHT REST IN THE PRESENCE OF CHRIST? HOW MIGHT YOUR DAILY OR WEEKLY ROUTINE CHANGE?

Day 19
THROUGH PAIN INTO REDEMPTION

J esus' work of redemption in our lives is often not an easy, straight-forward, or linear process.

This week, we have recalled the power of redemption in Jesus' life and teaching, and we have reoriented around the rest he provides by his grace. But as we reorient our hearts and minds around his ways, we have to remember that God's wisdom is higher than our understanding—and we will frequently be surprised by his roundabout, incremental ways of redemption.

As Bart Millard's wise manager, Brickell, told him in *I Can Only Imagine*, "Let your pain become your inspiration." Often, it's our trials, wounds, and failures that enable us to experience the greatest redemption.

JESUS' MYSTERIOUS WAYS

Throughout the gospel narratives, Jesus is full of surprises. Once, Jesus was walking with his disciples as they passed a fig tree (Matthew 21:18-22). Looking for something to eat, Jesus noticed the tree had nothing but leaves on it. "May you never bear fruit again!" he exclaims, and immediately the tree withered.

The disciples were shocked and confused. Why would Jesus curse a fig tree?

If we're honest, we often don't understand Jesus' ways. In him, freedom comes through obedience. In him, power comes through weakness. In him, life comes through death (John 11:25-26).

Just as the Israelites were made to wander for forty years in the wilderness prior to entering the Promised Land, God's people today often don't fully understand how the Lord is leading us in the moment.

It is not our job to know the times and ways of the Lord (Acts 1:7). "He changes times and seasons; he deposes kings and raises up others. He gives wisdom to the wise and knowledge to the discerning" (Daniel 2:21).

But instead of giving us an exact timeline of what will happen in our lives, he draws us into relationship and teaches us to trust him in all his ways.

THE LAST SUPPER

In Matthew 26, the Lord's last meal with his disciples is described in dramatic detail. When Jesus gave his disciples instructions for this meal's location, he leads them miraculously to a place they had never been (v. 18-19). When he said one of them would betray him, they didn't understand his words (v. 20-25). Even as he instituted a powerful, symbolic meal to re-enact his death and resurrection, they didn't fully understand (v. 26-29).

But when Jesus' followers looked back on that intimate meal, they realized the power and beauty of what they had experienced. He was preparing them, unbeknownst to them, for life without his physical presence.

Jesus' ways—even when not fully clear to us—are still sovereign and marvelous.

MYSTERIOUS WAYS, POWERFUL REDEMPTION

In *Imagine*, Bart's redemption occurred on several levels, over multiple years. He was reconciled to his father—who himself had experienced a transformation. He finally wrote from his heart—and the product was able to connect with others in a profound way. The failure he had previously experienced among producers was replaced by support from his heroes, Amy Grant and Michael W. Smith. And he reconciled with his longtime girlfriend.

In our lives, we often can't see what God is working at the time. Some have said God is weaving a beautiful tapestry in our lives. From our vantage point, it's a seemingly disconnected set of colors and thread. But when we get to see the final piece of art from his perspective, we see a beautiful pattern, woven through a careful, masterful process.

Whether we are in the light of a great season of intimacy with God or in the darkness of struggle, suffering, and confusion, God is with us. He has not left us alone. His ways are higher than our ways. His path may be long and winding, but it is the path that leads to glory.

When you lose sight of Jesus, remember Luke 21:28: "Stand up and lift up your heads, because your redemption is coming near." ■

STAND UP AND LIFT UP YOUR HEADS, BECAUSE YOUR *redemption* IS COMING NEAR.

LUKE 21:28

Questions for Reflection

Think about the ways in which God has worked in your life—through all the ups and downs.

IN THE SPACE ALLOWED, DRAW YOUR SPIRITUAL LIFE AS A PATH.

You could do this in two ways—or create your own way of illustrating your life. First, you could illustrate the path as it winds through different seasons of life, major events, or spiritual milestones. Second, you could chart your spiritual growth over time. What were the high points? When did you hit "rock bottom"?

Perhaps illustrating your life as a winding road or a roller coaster of progress will clarify how God has been leading you from beginning to end.

REFLECTING ON THE PICTURE, WHAT DO YOU NOTICE? WHAT NEW REFLECTIONS OR DISCOVERIES HAVE BEEN REVEALED? WHERE DO YOU SENSE GOD INVITING YOU TO FULLY TRUST HIM?

Light Shining Out of Darkness

Reflect on the powerful lyrics of this old hymn by William Cowper.

1. God moves in a mys-te-rious way His won-ders to per-form;
2. Deep in un-fath-om-a-ble mines of nev-er-fail-ing skill;
3. Ye fear-ful saints, fresh cour-age take; the clouds ye so much dread
4. Judge not the Lord by fee-ble sense, but trust Him for His grace;
5. His pur-pos-es will rip-en fast, un-fold-ing ev-'ry hour;
6. Blind un-be-lief is sure to err, and scan His work in vain;

He plants His foot-steps in the sea and rides up-on the storm.
He treas-ures up his bright de-signs, and works His sov-'reign will.
are big with mer-cy and shall break in bless-ings on your head.
be-hind a frown-ing prov-i-dence He hides a smil-ing face.
the bud may have a bit-ter taste, but sweet will be the flow'r.
God is His own in-ter-pret-er, and He will make it plain.

WORDS: William Cowper, 1774
MUSIC: *Scottish Psalter*, 1615

CM

JUDGE NOT
THE LORD BY
FEEBLE SENSE,

BUT TRUST
HIM FOR HIS
GRACE.

Day 20
SONGS OF REDEMPTION

Today and tomorrow, we will reimagine the power of a life of redemption. How might we envision and enact the way of radical forgiveness? Millions of people have been affected and inspired by Bart Millard's song "I Can Only Imagine." Songs have a way of connecting with both our minds and our hearts. Songs give language to our feelings and struggles. Songs allow us to use our bodies (including singing with our voices, raising our hands, or dancing) to connect with God in worship.

In fact, an entire book of the Bible is given to us as songs of redemption!

SONGS OF REDEMPTION

Jesus loved the Psalms. He pointed to Psalm 110 to describe his eternal authority (Matthew 22:41-46). He identified himself as the cornerstone Psalm 118 foreshadowed (Matthew 21:42). At the Last Supper, Jesus and his disciples sang a hymn based on Psalms 113-118 (Mark 14:26) In meeting with two men on the road to Emmaus, after his resurrection, he opened up the Scriptures to them—including the Psalms (Luke 24:44). On the Cross, he cried out in the language of Psalm 22 (Matthew 27:46).

One pastor and author has aptly described the Psalms as "the songs of Jesus."

Read through these Psalms and pray them (or sing them!) to the Lord in worship and gratitude. When we approach the Psalms, we don't merely read them, we pray them: "Search me and know me" (Psalm 139:23-24). Pray that the Lord would give you a spirit of worship as you praise him through these Psalms!

MAY THE WORDS OF MY MOUTH
   AND THE MEDITATION OF MY HEART
BE PLEASING IN YOUR SIGHT, LORD,
   MY ROCK AND MY REDEEMER.

– PSALM 19:14

NO ONE CAN REDEEM THE LIFE OF ANOTHER
   OR GIVE TO GOD A RANSOM FOR THEM—
BUT GOD WILL REDEEM ME FROM THE REALM OF THE DEAD;
   HE WILL SURELY TAKE ME TO HIMSELF

– PSALM 49:7,15

PRAISE THE LORD, MY SOUL;
  ALL MY INMOST BEING,
PRAISE HIS HOLY NAME.
PRAISE THE LORD, MY SOUL,
  AND FORGET NOT ALL HIS BENEFITS—
WHO FORGIVES ALL YOUR SINS
  AND HEALS ALL YOUR DISEASES,
WHO REDEEMS YOUR LIFE FROM THE PIT
  AND CROWNS YOU WITH LOVE AND COMPASSION,
WHO SATISFIES YOUR DESIRES WITH GOOD THINGS
  SO THAT YOUR YOUTH IS RENEWED LIKE THE EAGLE'S.
THE LORD WORKS RIGHTEOUSNESS
  AND JUSTICE FOR ALL THE OPPRESSED.

– PSALM 103:1-6

LET THE REDEEMED OF THE LORD TELL THEIR STORY—
  THOSE HE HAS REDEEMED FROM THE HAND OF THE FOE.

– PSALM 107:2

Questions for Reflection

At the beginning of our study, we read A. W. Tozer's statement, "What comes into our minds when we think about God is the most important thing about us." Having spent a whole week discovering redemption—and three weeks now walking with Jesus through the Gospels—

HOW WOULD YOU DESCRIBE GOD?

WHAT ATTRIBUTES OR CHARACTERISTICS BEST DESCRIBE GOD?

WHAT WORDS WOULD YOU USE TO DESCRIBE YOUR SALVATION?

WHAT WORDS DESCRIBE WHAT CHRIST HAS DONE FOR YOU?

HOW DO YOU WANT TO LIVE IN PRAISE AND LOVE FOR GOD—FATHER, SON, AND HOLY SPIRIT?

Day 21

CALL TO ACTION

O n the seventh day of each week, we're going to pause to review and reflect on the past week, and then we'll move forward with a Call to Action (see Introduction).

If you are behind a day or two, use this day to catch up. If you are caught up, use this day to review the previous six days' notes—especially all the Scripture references and stories.

Based on your week's reading and reflection, answer the following questions.

Recall

WHAT WAS THE MOST SIGNIFICANT THING YOU LEARNED ABOUT GOD THIS WEEK?

WHAT HAVE YOU LEARNED ABOUT YOURSELF THIS WEEK?

Reorient

WHAT WAS THE MOST SIGNIFICANT THING YOU LEARNED ABOUT THE CHRISTIAN LIFE THIS WEEK?

WHAT DOES IT LOOK LIKE TO REORIENT YOUR LIFE AROUND THE REALITY OF GOD AND HIS LOVE FOR YOU?

Reimagine

WHAT WOULD YOUR LIFE LOOK LIKE IF YOU FULLY BELIEVED EVERYTHING YOU READ THIS WEEK?

HOW MIGHT YOUR LIFE BE TOTALLY DIFFERENT AFTER A TRANSFORMATIVE EXPERIENCE WITH GOD?

Call To Action

In the space provided or in your own notebook, write a letter to Jesus. Recall how you lived before your redemption and the way he has changed your heart. Thank him from your heart for his nearness to you, for dying in your place on the Cross, for rising again in victory over death—so that you can be one with him for all eternity.

HOW DO YOU WANT TO EXPRESS YOUR GRATITUDE FOR CHRIST'S REDEMPTIVE WORK IN YOUR LIFE?

I Can Only Imagine

Verse 1

I CAN ONLY IMAGINE
WHAT IT WILL BE LIKE
WHEN I WALK,
BY YOUR SIDE
I CAN ONLY IMAGINE
WHAT MY EYES WILL SEE
WHEN YOUR FACE
IS BEFORE ME
I CAN ONLY IMAGINE
I CAN ONLY IMAGINE

Verse 2

I CAN ONLY IMAGINE
WHEN THAT DAY COMES
WHEN I FIND MYSELF
STANDING IN THE SON
I CAN ONLY IMAGINE
WHEN ALL I WILL DO IS FOREVER
FOREVER WORSHIP YOU
I CAN ONLY IMAGINE
I CAN ONLY IMAGINE

Chorus

SURROUNDED BY YOUR GLORY,
WHAT WILL MY HEART FEEL?
WILL I DANCE FOR YOU JESUS
OR IN AWE OF YOU BE STILL?
WILL I STAND IN YOUR PRESENCE
OR TO MY KNEES WILL I FALL?
WILL I SING HALLELUJAH,
WILL I BE ABLE TO SPEAK AT ALL?
I CAN ONLY IMAGINE
I CAN ONLY IMAGINE

IMAGINE

going home

Day 22

GOING HOME

What comes to your mind when you hear the word "home"?

Maybe you think of freshly baked cookies, fall backyard football games with your siblings and cousins, or large Thanksgiving gatherings.

But maybe you think of an unsafe place. Maybe you think of a demanding mother or an absent father. Perhaps your heart aches and your mind drifts to episodes of conflict, pain, and abuse.

Home is a loaded word. For almost all of us, home is complicated. Our memories are complex images of wholeness and brokenness, joy and hurt, safety and danger.

"I NEED TO GO HOME"

In *I Can Only Imagine*, Bart Millard stands in front of his band after a heartbreaking performance and significant rejection from record producers. He wants to quit, wants to hide, wants to get away from it all.

But he realizes that the producers' rejection of him is not the core issue—it only illuminates a long-neglected pain in his soul. Home, for Bart, is a painful memory. Home is not a place to retreat to, but a place to run from.

Standing in front of his band, he tells them, "I need to go home."

Often, we can only move forward in life by going backwards. We can only grow up by going home.

HOME MATTERS

We all long for home. We desire a true and better place of refuge—a safe space, a familiar and warm environment of care and security. Where does this deep longing come from?

In the Scriptures, places matter. The Bible takes careful note to record spaces and places in almost every book. Think about it:

When Abraham's wife Sarah died, he bought land from the Hittites and buried his wife Sarah in the cave in the field of Machpelah near Mamre (which is at Hebron) in the land of Canaan (Genesis 23:2, 19). Why are those geographical details included? Because, for Abraham, this is his beloved wife; these are the places captured in his memory alongside the memory of her; these places make up home for him.

HOME IN THE SCRIPTURES

The story of the Bible is a narrative that begins and ends at home.

But the Scriptures, both Old and New Testaments, carefully describe places as though they were intimately connected to the people and events that occurred there. The creation narrative is a beautiful telling of the beginning of the cosmos and then humanity, not as an entire, diverse race, but as a single man and woman in one unique home called Eden. Mankind is given dominion over the entire place of earth; by "ruling" over the land, animals, and seas, man images his Creator. But in their sin, the home of man, Eden, gives way to their "displacement"— from the presence of God and their home in Eden.

Through the rest of the Old Testament, home is a critically significant theme: Abel's punishment for murder is removal from his place in the land; Abraham is told by God to "go to a place I will show you"; slavery in Egypt is followed by the exodus into the wilderness, where the people wander in pursuit of the Promised Land; Israel's lowest points spiritually and morally lead them into exile in Babylon and other nations, their highest points see them restored to security in Jerusalem, the City of David, Zion itself!

Jesus' life and the narratives of the New Testament are equally full of references to significant places and reminders of home. We'll look at these throughout the week.

A powerful, hidden message of the Bible is this: We were each created by God with this divine capacity to fall in love with the natural spaces around us, for places to become home for us.

HOME IS A PLACE FULL OF MEANING

There is a difference between a space and a place. While space is all around us—it's air, ground, objects, and so on—some places are different. A place is a space that's infused with meaning. Place is unique; it's significant space, almost divine space. "Place is so fundamental to human existence and so ubiquitous that, paradoxically, it is easy to miss."

HOME IS NOT JUST A SPACE; IT'S A PLACE. HOME IS WHERE OUR HEART IS, WHERE WE FIND MEANING, WHERE WE ARE KNOWN, WHERE WE ARE SAFE, WHERE WE BELONG.

Home is hard to define but easy to describe. For me, home is where I grew up, in South Kansas City, on Cherry Street. Home is the campus of the University of Missouri, where I met my wife fifteen years ago. Home is where we now live in Columbia, Missouri with our three boys—with all the wonderful and broken things in our hearts, our relationships, and our physical house and yard. ■

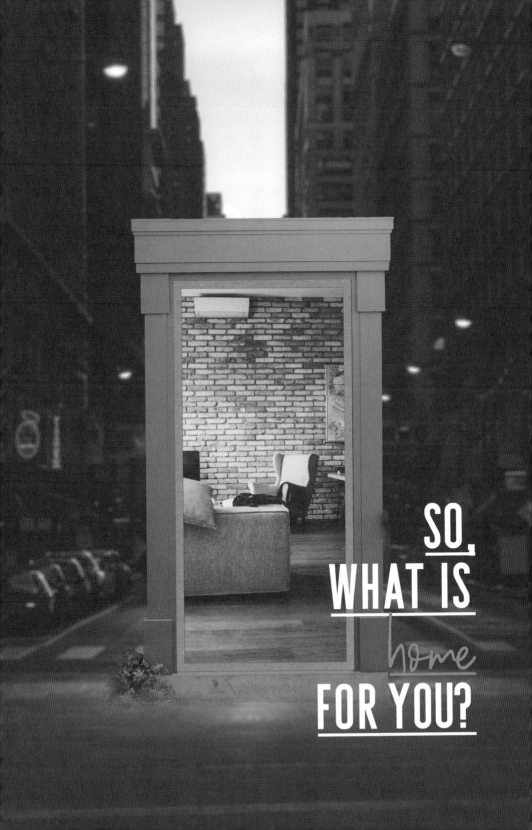

Questions for Reflection

Prayerfully reflect on and respond to the
following questions.

WHAT FIVE TO TEN WORDS COME INTO YOUR MIND WHEN YOU THINK ABOUT HOME?

WHAT THREE IMAGES REPRESENT HOME FOR YOU?

WHAT ONE MEMORY FROM THE FOLLOWING STAGES OF YOUR LIFE BEST REPRESENTS HOME?

AGE 6-11:

AGE 12-15:

AGE 16-18:

Day 23
LONGING FOR HOME

When Bart does return home, he is shocked by the changes that have occurred. Physical changes represent the spiritual transformation that have occurred in his father, Arthur.

Arthur's dilapidated house is bursting with life, with rooms being restored and walls being painted. Soon, even the old truck in the barn is restored, demonstrating further renewal in Arthur's life—and in the relationship of Bart and Arthur.

Not all stories of returning home have happy endings. But Bart and Arthur's lives represent the hope that no home is too broken and no life is worth leaving behind.

And in Bart's story and in ours, these places of significance to us—our home—are meaningful spaces where Jesus meets us, breathing transformation into the remarkably ordinary moments of life.

LONGING FOR HOME

We all long for home. Yesterday, we discovered this truth: We were each created by God with this divine capacity to fall in love with the natural spaces around us, for places to become home for us. And home is not just a space; it's a place. Home is where our heart is, where we find meaning, where we are known, where we are safe, where we belong.

Like Bart, we long to return home, but home may be complicated and painful. Like Bart, we long for a home where we are welcomed and received as we are. And like Bart, we may often struggle to accept this home, even when we do find it.

We all long for home, and the lack of a true home leaves us homesick. In her book, "Keeping Place: Reflections on the Meaning of Home," Jen Pollock Michel observes that in the eighteenth century homesickness was considered a legitimate source of physical illness and even a cause of death.

According to medical records, homesick patients experienced the symptoms of depression and fatigue, but they also suffered surprising physical symptoms, such as: sores, pustules, and fevers.

In several cases, sufferers refused to eat, growing so weak as to eventually die. Their doctors labeled their deaths severe cases of nostalgia—from nostos, "homecoming," and algia, "pain."

(The last mention of "nostalgia" on a death certificate was in 1918.)

In the hundreds of years since then—with all of our increases in medical technology and improved quality of life, with the ability to connect with people more easily through highways, affordable flight, and social media—has our generation become less homesick? It would be hard to support a hypothesis that we experience less homesickness. Instead, "to be human is to know the grief of some paradise lost…. Home represents humanity's most visceral ache—and our oldest desire."

Do you resonate with this? Do you feel homeless, displaced, and home-sick?

There's good news.

nos·tal·gia

//näˈstaljə//

noun

1. a sentimental longing or wistful affection for the past, typically for a period or place with happy personal associations

2. something done or presented in order to evoke feelings of nostalgia.

A HOME AWAITS US

As we discussed yesterday, the story of the Bible is a narrative that begins and ends at home.

We long for home because it was God's first gift to us and will be his last. "Because God's story begins in a garden and ends in a city, place isn't incidental to Christian hope, just as bodies aren't incidental to salvation."

In the gospel of John, Jesus' final words to his disciples are described in detail (John 13-17). Gathering before the Passover Festival in the upper room of a house in Jerusalem, Jesus encourages his disciples in the language of home.

Speaking of his own death, Jesus says,

> DO NOT LET YOUR HEARTS BE TROUBLED. YOU BELIEVE IN GOD; BELIEVE ALSO IN ME. MY FATHER'S HOUSE HAS MANY ROOMS; IF THAT WERE NOT SO, WOULD I HAVE TOLD YOU THAT I AM GOING THERE TO PREPARE A PLACE FOR YOU? AND IF I GO AND PREPARE A PLACE FOR YOU, I WILL COME BACK AND TAKE YOU TO BE WITH ME THAT YOU ALSO MAY BE WHERE I AM. YOU KNOW THE WAY TO THE PLACE I AM GOING.

> - JOHN 14:1-4

Jesus insisted on the permanence of his presence in the language of home. As Jesus says,

> I WILL NOT LEAVE YOU AS ORPHANS;
> I WILL COME TO YOU.... ANYONE WHO
> LOVES ME WILL OBEY MY TEACHING. MY
> FATHER WILL LOVE THEM, AND WE WILL
> COME TO THEM AND MAKE OUR HOME
> WITH THEM.
>
> - JOHN 14:18,23

We long for home because we were created for a true and eternal Home. In the promises of our Lord, a place has been prepared for us: A home, a beautiful and spacious house, is being made ready, and there are seats at the table for you and me.

In Christ, a Home awaits us. ■

WE WILL COME TO THEM & MAKE OUR *home* WITH THEM.

JOHN 14:23

Questions for Reflection

HOW DO YOU RELATE TO BART MILLARD'S FEARS IN GOING HOME? HOW DO YOU SEE YOUR OWN STORY IN BART'S (OR ARTHUR'S) STORY OF HOME?

HOW HAVE YOU SEEN A LONGING WITHIN YOURSELF FOR HOME? HOW HAVE YOU SEEN THIS LONGING MANIFESTED IN YOUR THOUGHTS, MEMORIES, AND HOPES?

JESUS HAS INVITED YOU HOME TO A LOVING FATHER, TO FORGIVENESS, AND TO REDEMPTION. HOW DOES HIS INVITATION SPEAK TO YOU TODAY? WHEN YOU THINK ABOUT A SEAT AT THE TABLE OF OUR FATHER'S HOUSE, HOW ARE YOU STRENGTHENED AND REASSURED FOR ALL YOU WILL FACE TODAY?

Day 24

FINDING HOME WITH JESUS

n Bart's story and in ours, the places of significance to us—our home—are meaningful spaces where we can find forgiveness and redemption in the remarkably ordinary moments of life. We long for this kind of home—where we find meaning, where we are known, where we are safe, where we belong.

Surely, there is hope for a home within this world. But even the best of homes in this lifetime are just a faint shadow of the true and better Home—the eternal place deep within all of our longings.

There is no discovering our true and eternal Home apart from Jesus Christ. Let's consider another story in our walk with him through the Gospels.

DISCOVERING HOME IN THE GOSPELS

Much like the Old Testament, the New Testament carefully notes the spaces and places of Jesus' life, the disciples' journeys, and the apostles' missionary travels. As soon as we determine to walk with Jesus in the Gospels, we are welcomed into an ancient world of meaningful places.

When Matthew, Mark, Luke, and John introduce us to Jesus, we find him walking along the paths of Galilee, sitting in Jerusalem's town square, eating with tax collectors and sinners in Capernaum, and reclining in the upper room with his disciples. In the final moments before his arrest, trial, and crucifixion, he collapses in the Garden of Gethsemane. All four ospel writers take careful

note of the places surrounding Jesus' life on earth. These places matter!

When he was crucified, it was carried out, quite significantly, "outside the city gate" (Hebrews 13:12). Christ's great victory, of course, is his physical, literal, bodily resurrection. Jesus doesn't achieve victory over the material world and then return with only a spiritual existence. No, in his perfection and eternal life, Jesus has a body that exists in space and time, that could still eat (John 21:1-13), walk (Luke 24:13-35), and lead his disciples to the Mount of Olives for his ascension (Acts 1:12).

Jesus' literal, physical resurrection and ascension—he lives and reigns within a human body and a finite place—means that no physical space lacks meaning. The fact that Jesus' eternal life is physical means that Home is more than a symbol; it's a real place of spiritual power.

In his earthly life and ministry, Jesus didn't have a home (Matthew 8:20), and yet everywhere he went became home for those around him. In a very real sense, Home is wherever Christ is.

HOME IS WHEREVER CHRIST MEETS US.

GOING HOME

So, again, I ask: What is Home for you?

Perhaps it's time to return home. Maybe it's time to come home to yourself—to who God has made you to be. Maybe it's a good time to return to your physical home or neighborhood and explore memories.

Or maybe, in a spiritual sense, it's time to find a home in Christ and rest in his eternal presence.

AT HOME WITH JESUS

Recall the short story from Luke 10: Jesus and his disciples were traveling when Martha invited them into her home. As Jesus and the disciples relaxed in the living room, Martha went about preparing the meal. Picking out ingredients, kneading the dough, preparing the entrée and sides, and scrubbing dishes, Martha was exhausted.

In the midst of her hard work, Martha doesn't miss the fact that her sister, Mary, isn't helping. Instead, Mary is spread out on the floor, relaxing with Jesus and their friends. Mary wasn't worried about the meal or the table or the dishes.

Martha, in her frustration, asks Jesus to rebuke her sister for her—passive-aggressive request. But Jesus' response extends even to us today:

"MARTHA, MARTHA," THE LORD ANSWERED, "YOU ARE WORRIED AND UPSET ABOUT MANY THINGS, BUT FEW THINGS ARE NEEDED—OR INDEED ONLY ONE. MARY HAS CHOSEN WHAT IS BETTER, AND IT WILL NOT BE TAKEN AWAY FROM HER"

- LUKE 10:40-42

Imagine Jesus speaking these words to you. Put your name in the place of Martha's name. "My friend," Jesus says to you, "you are worried about much, but only one thing matters: Being with me!"

Only in Christ do we find a home without demands, heavy burdens, and expectations. Only at home with Jesus are we able to be ourselves, to put our work down, and to spread out on a comfortable rug to listen to the stories, jokes, and invitations of our Lord.

Jesus' words to Martha and Mary tell us that we don't have to be homeless in this world. Wherever Jesus is, we find Home. What we need most is not the right house, newer furniture, or an Instagram-worthy meal prepared in a Pinterest-worthy kitchen.

We need to relax at Home with Jesus. Only one thing is needed. ■

HE INVITES YOU
TO COME
home

Questions for Reflection

WHY DO YOU THINK THE GOSPEL WRITERS ARE SO CAREFUL TO DESCRIBE THE PHYSICAL PLACES AND LOCATIONS WHERE JESUS LIVED, WALKED, AND MINISTERED? HOW DOES THIS AFFECT THE WAY YOU THINK ABOUT THE PLACES AND LOCATIONS IN YOUR LIFE—YOUR NEIGHBORHOOD, LOCAL COFFEE SHOP, PLACE OF EMPLOYMENT, AND CHURCH BUILDING?

IMAGINE SITTING DOWN AT YOUR OWN HOME WITH JESUS. HOW DOES HIS PRESENCE TRANSFORM YOUR HOUSE? IF JESUS CAME TO YOUR HOME FOR DINNER, WHAT WOULD YOUR PRIORITY BE—TO PREPARE THE RIGHT MEAL OR TO ENJOY HIS PRESENCE?

JESUS HAS INVITED YOU INTO HIS HOME. IN THE PRESENCE OF THE KING, WHAT IS THE ONE THING YOU NEED? WHAT DOES IT LOOK LIKE TO LET JESUS BE YOUR HOME?

Day 25

HOME BEYOND THE GRAVE (PART 1)

This week, we have recalled the importance of home from the Old and New Testaments. We have also completed some exercises and reflection questions on our own personal experience of home.

Now, our task is to reorient around a new sense of home (and then to reimagine life with God in the reality of a permanent, eternal Home). To do so, let's recall another story of Jesus in the Gospels and allow it to transform the meaning of home for us.

THE WAY HOME

As we reflect on the meaning of home for us as Christians, consider this question:

How do we get Home?

I don't just mean how we get to our childhood home, or to a place of safety and meaning in this world. How do we get to our final and eternal Home?

Another way to ask the question is, how do we find a Home beyond the grave?

One day, Jesus was ministering with his disciples when their friend, Mary, approached him with bad news. Lazarus, Mary's brother and Jesus' close friend, was dangerously sick. John 11 notes that Jesus loved Lazarus—and Mary and her sister, Martha (v. 5). And yet, Jesus didn't leave to see Lazarus.

In fact, Jesus stayed where he was for two more days. Why? He loves Lazarus. Why does he wait?

Maybe this resonates with you: Why does the Lord not answer me right away? Why do my prayers seem to go unanswered? Why does the Lord seem absent when I need him most? I thought he loved me!

When Jesus finally moves toward the town of Bethany, Lazarus is already dead—he's been in the grave for four days (v. 17). Along the road, Martha meets him and blames Jesus.

> "IF YOU HAD BEEN HERE, MY BROTHER WOULDN'T HAVE DIED!"
>
> - v. 21

She's heartbroken. She's angry. She's confused. It doesn't add up. Why would the Lord—who has the power to heal—let her brother die? Why would a good and loving God allow so much pain?

When Jesus reaches Bethany, Martha's sister, Mary, approaches him with the same statement. "If you had been here, my brother wouldn't have died!" (v. 32).

HOPE BEYOND THE GRAVE

But Jesus isn't cold-hearted. The text says he is "deeply moved in spirit and troubled" (v. 33). That phrase in the original Greek means something similar to upset in his stomach, groaning in pain, or overwhelmed with grief. Seeing Lazarus's family members grieve, Jesus begins to weep (v. 35).

Too often, we think of Jesus as only a spiritual being without regular human emotions, but when he took on flesh he was the most fully human person to ever live. He had emotions, he felt things, he had desires, he experienced things—all without sin.

We see, in Christ, the most loyal, compassionate, and loving man who ever lived. He was fully human, and wasn't afraid to weep openly at the death of a friend. In his tears, we find that our pain, our sadness over death are not foreign to him. To be fully human is to mourn and grieve deeply. We live in a world wrecked by sin and death, and at our core, we are restless and weary with suffering.

If you recognize what's happening here, Jesus is arriving to a funeral. People have gathered—they were waiting for Jesus to come. Lazarus is in the tomb, buried, three days and nights in the ground, and people gather to hear what Jesus is going to say.

Speaking to the crowd that had gathered, Jesus says, "I am the resurrection and the life. The one who believes in me will live, even though they die; and whoever lives by believing in me will never die" (v. 25-26).

Only Jesus could arrive at a funeral and announce, "Whoever believes in me will live—even though they die!" Because only Jesus had authority over life and death, over heaven and earth (Matthew 28:18).

Then turning to the tomb, Jesus calls out in a loud voice, "Lazarus, come out!" (v. 43). And then the unthinkable: "The dead man came out, his hands and feet wrapped with strips of linen, and a cloth around his face" (v. 44). And before the speechless crowd, Jesus says—I can imagine a smile on his face—"Take off the grave clothes and let him go" (v. 45).

Jesus is the resurrection and the life. Whoever believes in him will live—even though we die. ■

IN CHRIST, THERE IS A HOPE
STRONGER THAN DEATH.

AND IF THERE IS A HOPE
BEYOND THE GRAVE,
THERE IS ALSO A

home

BEYOND THE GRAVE.

Questions for Reflection

HOW HAVE YOU EXPERIENCED HOMESICKNESS IN YOUR LIFE? HOW ARE YOU CURRENTLY FEELING IT?

WHAT IS MOST POWERFUL ABOUT THIS RESURRECTION NARRATIVE TO YOU? HOW DO YOU FIND HOPE AND LIFE IN THE RESURRECTION OF LAZARUS AND IN THE RESURRECTION THAT IT POINTS TO, JESUS CHRIST'S?

IMAGINE ATTENDING THIS FUNERAL SERVICE. HEAVY WITH EMOTION, YOU SEE JESUS ARRIVE AND BEGIN TO WEEP. HOW DOES HIS EMOTION FREE YOU TO EMBRACE YOUR DEEPEST FEELINGS AND LONGINGS? HOW DOES HIS MESSAGE OF LIFE—SPEAKING NEW LIFE INTO THE TOMB—BRING JOY TO YOUR HEART?

Day 26

HOME BEYOND THE GRAVE (PART 2)

Yesterday, we began the task of reorienting around a new sense of home. In doing so, we began with the story of Jesus attending Lazarus's funeral service; seeking to understand life, death, and the true meaning of home for us.

Remember, the question that began our journey in John 11 was, How do we find a Home beyond the grave?

HOME BEYOND THE GRAVE

The resurrection of Lazarus reminds us that if we have a hope beyond the grave, we also have a home beyond the grave.

Jesus raised Lazarus to new life as a physical demonstration of a spiritual reality. In Christ, there is a life bigger than death, a hope that no funeral can diminish. "He who believes in me will live, even though he dies." Jesus doesn't promise to raise us back to physical life—even Lazarus himself would die again. But Jesus promises that he will raise all who believe to a new spiritual life. This is not just life after death; it's life through death.

Jesus spoke of death in this passage, and he would later have to taste it himself. He experienced death in our place—taking our sins onto himself—so that his righteousness could be given to us. Having authority over life and death as the Creator of all things, Jesus didn't stay in the tomb any longer than Lazarus. On the third day, his stone was rolled back and a dead man got up and took off his grave clothes.

What does all this mean for us? Just as Lazarus was raised, just as Jesus was raised once and for all, so we have a hope of physical resurrection and eternal life.

We have the hope of a real, physical existence beyond death!

YOUR EXILE HAS COME TO AN END

Consider another scene from Jesus' life. Early in his earthly ministry, well before he was a popular and controversial figure in Judea, Jesus was attending a Sabbath-day worship gathering in his hometown's local synagogue (Luke 4:14-30).

Jesus offered to read the day's Scripture, and the priest handed him a scroll from the book of Isaiah. Standing up in the presence of his family members, childhood friends, and many familiar townsfolk, Jesus opened to Isaiah 61:1-2 and began to read:

THE SPIRIT OF THE LORD IS ON ME, BECAUSE HE HAS ANOINTED ME TO PROCLAIM GOOD NEWS TO THE POOR. HE HAS SENT ME TO PROCLAIM FREEDOM FOR THE PRISONERS AND RECOVERY OF SIGHT FOR THE BLIND, TO SET THE OPPRESSED FREE, TO PROCLAIM THE YEAR OF THE LORD'S FAVOR.

- LUKE 4:18-19

Sitting down, with the eyes of the room fixed on him, Jesus spoke again. "Today this Scripture has been fulfilled in your hearing" (v. 21).

Today, this Scripture has been fulfilled. Today, in Christ, your imprisonment has come to an end. Today, in Christ, your sight has been restored. Today, in Christ, your exile has come to an end.

At the end of the age, God will resurrect our bodies and bring us home. Just as Jesus declared to the crowd gathered at Lazarus's funeral service, whoever believes in Christ will live forever—even though we die. We will live forever because Jesus has come. We have a home forever because Jesus has declared an end to our exile.

In Jesus Christ, homesickness is put in its grave. ■

IN OTHER WORDS:

IT'S TIME TO RETURN

home

Questions for Reflection

Imagine now that you are Lazarus: You wake up in a dark grave, wrapped in linen strips and the thick scent of decay, yet your eyes are open. There's an opening in the tomb—the stone has been rolled back. You get up and walk out, into the light, and into the arms of Jesus.

WHAT WOULD THAT EXPERIENCE BE LIKE?

JESUS ANNOUNCED THE END OF OUR EXILE; IT'S TIME TO RETURN HOME. HOW HAVE YOU EXPERIENCED HOMESICKNESS AS A TYPE OF EXILE IN YOUR LIFE? HOW DO JESUS' WORDS ENCOURAGE YOU?

HOW OFTEN DO YOU THINK ABOUT DEATH? HOW DO YOU FEEL ABOUT IT? HOW DOES IT REORIENT YOUR THOUGHTS AND FEELINGS THAT JESUS SPEAKS TO YOU: WHOEVER BELIEVES IN ME WILL LIVE—EVEN THOUGH YOU DIE?

Day 27

OUR HAPPY ENDING

I n the days after Arthur's death, Bart's heart has been transformed. He has gone home, and God has worked a beautiful redemption—both in Arthur's life and in Bart's life.

BART'S HAPPY ENDING

Returning to tour on the bus, Bart can't sleep. Taking up his pen in a moment of clarity, he writes a short, simple song that would change the lives of millions of people.

In the climactic moment of *I Can Only Imagine*, Bart is asked to come before a standing-room-only crowd to perform "I Can Only Imagine."

To the delight of the crowd, Bart's performance shines. The song connects to the deep places of the audience's longing for a loving Father, for forgiveness, for redemption, and for a final home-coming.

Embracing the longtime love of his life, Shannon, Bart gets his happy ending. "I Can Only Imagine" becomes one of the most popular and far-reaching songs in contemporary history, and millions today continue to worship to its tune.

Why does this moment resonate with us so deeply? We all long for a happy ending.

OUR HAPPY ENDING

Two of the most prominent writers of the twentieth century, J.R.R. Tolkien (author of *The Lord of the Rings* series) and C.S. Lewis (author of the *Chronicles of Narnia* and *Mere Christianity*), were close friends and taught together at Oxford in England.

Despite the popular success of their books, many scholars rejected their books as fairy tales disconnected from reality. One set of critics said Tolkien and Lewis were "guilty of the heresy of the Happy Ending."

Indeed, they were guilty of the Happy Ending. Tolkien and Lewis identified as Christians and wrote from a Christian worldview. And they didn't view the genre of fairy tale as a worthless pursuit. Instead, they believed that the fairy tale ending was the most accurate way to tell a true story.

In *The Lord of the Rings* and *Narnia*, Tolkien and Lewis crafted compelling stories based on the biblical hope that redemption was coming, and God's people would one day experience a happy ending. Through stories of hobbits and a ring, beavers and a lion, these authors told the story of home in a breathtakingly biblical images. One day, the great struggle will end, winter will give way to spring, and our King will return.

Let the critics say what they will:

WE ARE A PEOPLE OF FAIRY TALE ENDINGS.

When we reach the last page of the book and the movie credits roll up the screen, God's people will indeed live happily ever after. We will be Home.

Indeed, we can only imagine what it will be like. ■

Questions for Reflection

WHAT ASPECT OF BART'S STORY CONNECTS MOST DEEPLY WITH YOUR OWN STORY? WHAT PART OF HIS HAPPY ENDING DO YOU LONG TO EXPERIENCE?

WE HAVE SPENT FOUR WEEKS TOGETHER, WALKING WITH JESUS THROUGH THE GOSPELS. WHICH STORIES AND NARRATIVES COME TO MEMORY? WHAT SCENES FROM JESUS' LIFE REMAIN MOST POWERFUL TO YOU?

JESUS HAS INVITED YOU TO A LOVING FATHER, TO FORGIVENESS, TO REDEMPTION, AND TO COME HOME. REFLECTING ON *I CAN ONLY IMAGINE* AND THE NARRATIVES OF JESUS' LIFE, DEATH, AND RESURRECTION, HOW DO YOU NOW ANSWER THE QUESTION: WHAT DOES IT LOOK LIKE TO LET GOD BE YOUR HOME?

Day 28
CALL TO ACTION

O n the seventh day of each week, we're going to pause to review and reflect on the past week, and then we'll move forward with a Call to Action (see Introduction).

If you are behind a day or two, use this day to catch up. If you are caught up, use this day to review the previous six days' notes—especially all the Scripture references and stories.

Based on your week's reading and reflection, answer the following questions.

Recall

WHAT WAS THE MOST SIGNIFICANT THING YOU LEARNED ABOUT GOD THIS WEEK?

WHAT HAVE YOU LEARNED ABOUT YOURSELF THIS WEEK?

Reorient

WHAT WAS THE MOST SIGNIFICANT THING YOU LEARNED ABOUT THE
CHRISTIAN LIFE THIS WEEK?

WHAT DOES IT LOOK LIKE TO REORIENT YOUR LIFE AROUND THE
REALITY OF GOD AND HIS LOVE FOR YOU?

Reimagine

WHAT WOULD YOUR LIFE LOOK LIKE IF YOU FULLY BELIEVED
EVERYTHING YOU READ THIS WEEK?

HOW MIGHT YOUR LIFE BE TOTALLY DIFFERENT AFTER A
TRANSFORMATIVE EXPERIENCE WITH GOD?

Call To Action

In the space provided or in your own notebook, write a letter to God, your heavenly Father.

Recall how you lived before your redemption and the way he has changed your heart. Thank him from your heart for sending Jesus Christ to live, die, and rise again in your place—so that you can be one with him for all eternity. In this letter, describe the Home that you long for in him. Ask him to transform the memory of home for you, and imagine—in your own written words—what it will be like to spend eternity by his side, with his face before you.

AS YOU'VE PROGRESSED THROUGH THE LAST FOUR WEEKS OF THIS STUDY,

you probably experienced a range of emotions, questions, convictions, and hopes.

And now, as you return to your normal life, what will you do next?

Here's a challenge: Take a season to pray, listen, and act. Ask God to show you His immeasurable goodness and glory, and move forward with a brighter, more steadfast faith.

Rest in Jesus. Explore the depths of His wisdom and knowledge. Follow Him wherever He leads you.

As a final reflection, consider these words from Romans 11:33-36, and experience the fullness of His riches in your life.

> 33 Oh, the depth of the riches of the wisdom and knowledge of God!
> How unsearchable his judgments,
> and his paths beyond tracing out!
> 34 "Who has known the mind of the Lord?
> Or who has been his counselor?"
> 35 "Who has ever given to God,
> that God should repay them?"
> 36 For from him and through him and for him are all things.
> To him be the glory forever! Amen.

REFERENCES

WEEK ONE

Page 18: See Appendix: Reading the Gospels as Stories.

Page 23: A.W. Tozer, Knowledge of the Holy.

Page 30: David Blankenhorn, Fatherless in America, 1.

Page 31: Douglas Wilson, Father Hunger.

Page 32: Mike Wilkerson, Redemption, 51.

Page 33: Douglas Wilson, Father Hunger, 2.

Page 45: Stuart Townsend, "How Deep the Father's Love for Us."

Page 49: Tim Keller, "Bathed in Blessing" Sermon at Redeemer Presbyterian Church, October 2, 2011.

WEEK TWO

Page 78-79: Mark Berman, "I forgive you. Relatives of the Charleston church shooting victims address Dylann Roof." The Washington Post. June 19, 2015.

Page 79: Bob Smietana, "A year later, families of the Charleston shooting still wrestle with forgiveness." The Washington Post. June 17, 2016.

WEEK THREE

Page 114: See also, Jeremy Linneman, Life-Giving Groups: How to Grow Healthy, Multiplying Community Groups, pp. 16-18.

Page 114: Chester, A Meal with Jesus: Discovering Grace, Community and Mission Around the Table, 10.

Page 115: Chester, A Meal with Jesus, 13.

Page 115: Chester, A Meal with Jesus.

Page 115: Robert J. Karris, Eating Your Way through Luke's Gospel (Order of Saint Benedict, 2006).

Page 121: Koren Talmud Bavli, Vol. 2-3, Tractate Shabbat; see especially, "Thirty-Nine Creative Activities" prohibited.

Page 136: L. Michael Morales, "Jesus and the Psalms." The Gospel Coalition. April 11, 2011.

Page 136: Timothy J. Keller and Kathy Keller, The Songs of Jesus: A Year of Daily Devotions in the Psalms.

WEEK FOUR

Page 148: See Jeremy Linneman, "Rooted: Pastoral Reflections on Place." jslinneman.com/2016/07/22/rooted-pastoral-reflections-on-place

Page 148: Craig G Bartholomew, Where Mortals Dwell: A Christian View of Place for Today.

Page 153: Jen Pollock Michel, Keeping Place: Reflections on the Meaning of Home, 27.

Page 155: Michel, 27-28.

Page 155: Michel, 33.

Page 179: Michel, 39.

I CAN ONLY

One Unimaginable Journey

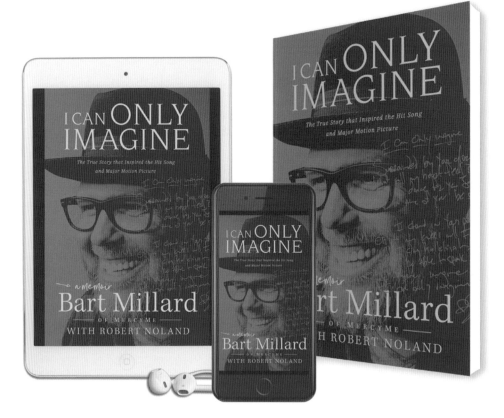

For the first time, MercyMe's Bart Millard puts pen to paper to share the true story behind the song that inspired the world.

IMAGINE

Encourage your child's sense of wonder and faith

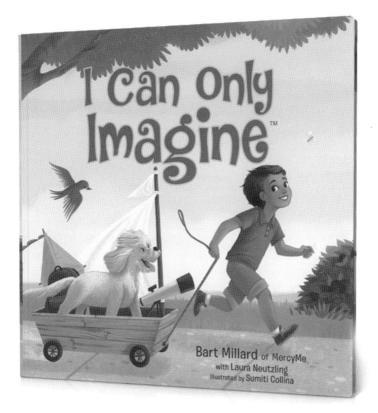

Resources for your whole family

PICTURE BOOK is for ages 4-8 years (ISBN 9781400321339)

BOARD BOOK is for ages 0-4 years (ISBN 9781400322015)

THE
I CAN ONLY IMAGINE
LEATHER
NOTEBOOK

HANDCRAFTED WITH THE HIGHEST QUALITY MATERIALS

Carefully made by hand in Haiti, this refillable notebook helps to create sustainable and dignified employment. 100% vegetable-tanned leather creates a rich color and soft texture. Includes the new City on a Hill Notebook, a high-quality 128-page lined book — printed in the USA.

ABOUT THE AUTHOR
Jeremy Linneman

Jeremy Linneman, M.A., is lead pastor of Trinity
Community Church in Columbia, Missouri. Prior to planting
Trinity, he served as a staff pastor of Sojourn Community
Church in Louisville, Kentucky for seven years.

Jeremy frequently writes, speaks and consults with
churches of all sizes on discipleship, small groups and
leadership development. His resources are available at
jslinneman.com. He and his wife, Jessie, have three sons and
spend most of their free time outdoors.

PRAY. THINK. CREATE.

IMAGINE.